The Land and People of

FRANCE

The Land and People of®

FRANCE

by *Jonathan Harris*

J. B. LIPPINCOTT   NEW YORK

Country maps by Eric Elias.

Historical maps adapted from: Colin McEvedy, *Century World History Factfinder* (London: Century Hutchinson Publishing Group Ltd.).

THE LAND AND PEOPLE OF
is a registered trademark of
Harper & Row, Publishers, Inc.

The Land and People of France
Copyright © 1989 by Jonathan Harris
Printed in the U.S.A. All rights reserved.
For information address J. B. Lippincott Junior Books,
10 East 53rd Street, New York, N.Y. 10022.

Library of Congress Cataloging-in-Publication Data
Harris, Jonathan.
    The land and people of France / by Jonathan Harris
        p.   cm. — (Portraits of the nations series)
    Rev. ed. of : The land and people of France / by Lillian
J. Bragdon. Rev. ed. 1972.
    Bibliography: p.
    Filmography: p.
    Discography: p.
    Includes index.
    Summary: Introduces the history, geography, people, culture,
government, and economy of this European country that has
made contributions to western civilization and is undergoing
significant social and economic changes.
    ISBN 0-397-32320-4 : $ ISBN 0-397-32321-2 (lib. bdg.) : $
    1. France—Juvenile literature. [1. France.] I. Bragdon,
Lillian J. Land and people of France. II. Title. III. Series.
DC18.H36   1989   88-19211
944—dc 19   CIP
                                                              AC

10 9 8 7 6 5 4 3 2 1
First Edition

Contents

THE WORLD

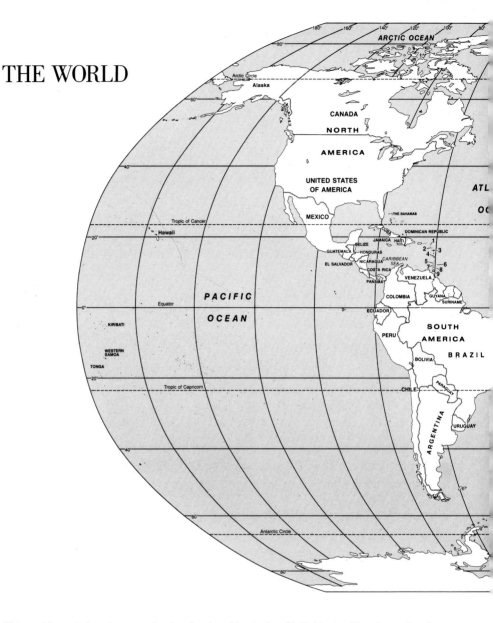

This world map is based on a projection developed by Arthur H. Robinson. The shape of each country and its size, relative to other countries, are more accurately expressed here than in previous maps. The map also gives equal importance to all of the continents, instead of placing North America at the center of the world. *Used by permission of the Foreign Policy Association.*

Legend

—— International boundaries

·········· Disputed or undefined boundaries

Projection: Robinson

| 0 | 1000 | 2000 | 3000 Miles |

| 0 | 1000 | 2000 | 3000 Kilometers |

Caribbean Nations

1. Anguilla
2. St. Christopher and Nevis
3. Antigua and Barbuda
4. Dominica
5. St. Lucia
6. Barbados
7. St. Vincent
8. Grenada
9. Trinidad and Tobago

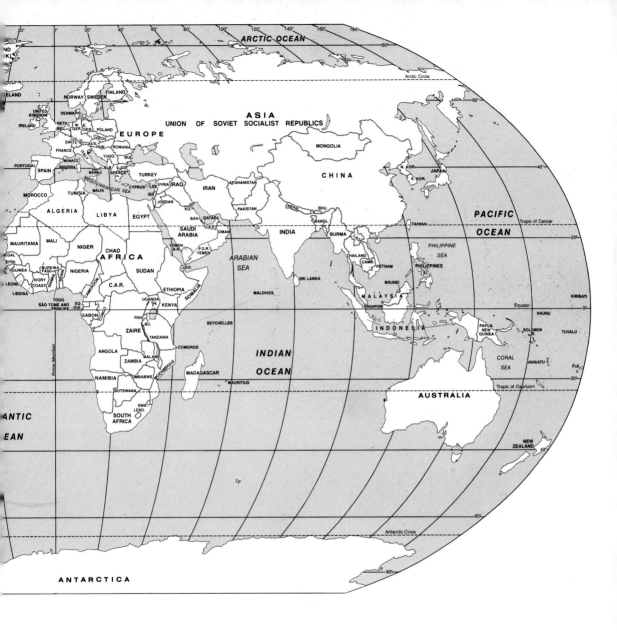

Abbreviations

ALB.	—Albania	C.A.R.	—Central African Republic	LEB.	—Lebanon	RWA.	—Rwanda
AUS.	—Austria	CZECH.	—Czechoslovakia	LESO.	—Lesotho	S. KOR.	—South Korea
BANGL.	—Bangladesh	DJI.	—Djibouti	LIE.	—Liechtenstein	SWA.	—Swaziland
BEL.	—Belgium	E.GER.	—East Germany	LUX.	—Luxemburg	SWITZ.	—Switzerland
BHU.	—Bhutan	EQ. GUI.	—Equatorial Guinea	NETH.	—Netherlands	U.A.E.	—United Arab Emirates
BU.	—Burundi	GUI. BIS.	—Guinea Bissau	N. KOR.	—North Korea	W. GER.	—West Germany
BUL.	—Bulgaria	HUN.	—Hungary	P.D.R.–YEMEN	—People's Democratic	YEMEN A.R.	—Yemen Arab Republic
CAMB.	—Cambodia	ISR.	—Israel		Republic of Yemen	YUGO.	—Yugoslavia

NOTE ON CURRENCY EXCHANGE RATES

The exchange rates for francs and dollars used throughout this book are approximately those that prevailed while it was being written: 6 francs = $1, or 16.7 cents = 1 franc.

Mini Facts

OFFICIAL NAME: French Republic *(République Française)*

LOCATION: Situated in western Europe, with the Atlantic Ocean to the west, the English Channel to the northwest, Belgium to the north, West Germany and Luxembourg to the northeast, Switzerland to the east, Italy to the southeast, the Mediterranean Sea to the south, and Spain to the southwest.

AREA: 212,918 square miles (551,602 square kilometers)

CAPITAL: Paris

POPULATION: 55,506,000 (1987 est.)

MAJOR LANGUAGE: French

RELIGIONS: Roman Catholicism, Protestantism, Judaism, Islam

TYPE OF GOVERNMENT: Republic

HEAD OF STATE: President (7-year term)

HEAD OF GOVERNMENT: Prime Minister

PARLIAMENT: National Assembly (491 members, 5-year terms)
Senate (322 senators, 9-year terms)

ADULT LITERACY: 99 percent (1980)

LIFE EXPECTANCY: Female, 78; Male, 70 (1986)

MAIN PRODUCTS: *Agriculture*—cereal grains, dairy products, beef, sugar beets, potatoes, wine grapes. *Manufacturing and processing*—aircraft, automobiles, armaments, electronic and telecommunications equipment, steel products, chemicals, textiles, clothing, wine, perfume. *Mining and drilling*—iron ore, coal, bauxite, uranium, natural gas.

CHAPTER I

France's Finest Hour— And Her Darkest

Working swiftly and skillfully, the French Resistance fighter shaped the plastic explosive to fit the railroad track. He pressed the soft material tightly against the rail so that it could not be detected from above. Then he inserted the fuse and set it to go off the instant a train rumbled over it. When all was ready he called in his lookouts, the men who were guarding against any unexpected appearance of a German patrol.

The men raced to the car waiting for them on the road nearby. It zoomed off—no hanging around to enjoy the explosion. Better be out of the area before it happened.

They had barely made their escape when a train chugged into view. The long line of flatcars carried German tanks, heavy guns, and trucks. On the first car, the middle car, and the last car, German guards manned machine guns.

The locomotive almost leaped into the air as the explosive ripped the track. The other cars tumbled and jackknifed in crazy patterns. The heavy cargo crashed off the cars to the ground, some of the huge pieces landing upside down, others on their sides.

The embattled German armies needed these tanks and guns desperately but would not get them for many days. The French Resistance had done its job.

Hundreds of miles away, in southern France, four men wearing peasant clothes followed a woman out of the woods. She was no ordinary peasant but the leader of a nationwide underground network that rescued Allied airmen and escaped prisoners of war. The four men were Americans. They were all that remained of the crew of a B-17 bomber that had been shot down. They had managed to escape capture. Now they had made contact with the Resistance.

Moving cautiously in the predawn darkness, the airmen followed their guide to an isolated farmhouse. The woman knocked, heard a whispered challenge, whispered a password. The door opened, and the group disappeared inside.

Within days the Americans were passed along from that secret hiding place to another. Eventually they were escorted out of German-occupied France and made their way back to England. There their precious combat skills could once again be put to good use.

By the end of the war, about 3,000 British, French, American, and other airmen had been saved in this way. Thousands of other fighting men and a large number of political prisoners were also led to freedom.

A secret fighting organization could not be set up easily or quickly. The Resistance had to be built slowly, carefully, through many months of planning and preparation.

It started soon after June 22, 1940, one of the blackest days in French history. That was the day when a stunned and humiliated France signed the harsh surrender terms imposed by the victorious Germans. It marked the end of six terrifying weeks, during which Hitler's rampaging armored divisions and bomber fleets had shattered the allied French and British armies. The British had gathered up some of their troops and had retreated to their island kingdom.

The first call for resistance went out a few days before the surrender was signed. It came from a then little-known French general named Charles de Gaulle. He had commanded one of the few French tank units to carry out successful attacks against the Germans. When the rest of the French army went into full retreat, de Gaulle refused to accept the idea of surrender. He escaped to England.

On June 18, 1940, de Gaulle issued his historic rallying cry to his conquered countrymen. "France has lost a battle," he told them via British radio,

but France has not lost the war! . . . Must we abandon all hope? Is our defeat final? To those questions I answer—No! Whatever happens, the flame of French resistance must not and shall not be extinguished!

There were French patriots who needed no more encouragement. In scattered and spontaneous individual actions, they began to resist the occupation. At first it might be only a *Vive la France!* scribbled on a stone wall. Or perhaps it was a shrug of the shoulder and a refusal to answer when addressed by a German soldier. Here and there a German army telephone wire might be cut.

Soon the resistants began to seek each other out. They organized themselves into groups, reached out to other groups, formed networks. Gradually their actions grew bolder, more confident, more united.

As Resistance actions multiplied, the penalties imposed by the Germans grew increasingly drastic. At first there were only fines for defacing German propaganda posters or scribbling anti-Nazi graffiti. Men and women who carried out sabotage were sent to prison. Often the town they lived in had to pay a heavy fine.

It soon became obvious that such measures could not stop the Resistance. The Nazis switched to a policy of executing hostages. In the beginning, one hostage would be executed for every Resistance action, or for every German killed. But the number of executions escalated swiftly from one for one to ten for one, twenty for one, and more. For example: on October 21, 1941, a Resistant shot and killed the commander of German forces in the seaport of Nantes. Three days later, the Germans shot forty-eight French hostages.

There were those who blamed the Resistance instead of the Germans for these reprisals. They felt it was best to get along with the occupying forces and that the Resistance fighters were irresponsible troublemakers. Such people informed on the Resistance whenever they could. Many Resistance networks were shattered as a result, with thousands of Resistants captured.

The captured fighters fell into the hands of the dreaded Gestapo, the German secret police. Gestapo officers quickly became notorious for using barbarous forms of torture to extract information. They tortured and then executed an estimated 25,000 Resistants. About 200,000 more were shipped off to concentration camps, where half of them died.

At the end of the war the Allies hunted down many of these Gestapo torturers for trial as war criminals. Many escaped, the largest number finding refuge in South America. But a few of them, possessing special knowledge or skills, were secretly employed as Allied intelligence agents operating against the Soviets. Later, when their usefulness was ended or when they were in danger of exposure, the Allies helped them to get away.

One of these was Klaus Barbie, former Gestapo commander in Lyons. He was high up on the list of most wanted ex-Nazis. Infamous for his merciless treatment of captured Resistants, he was known as the

Butcher of Lyons. Above all, he had surpassed all bounds in his deliberate brutality against Jean Moulin. Moulin was the man whom de Gaulle had personally entrusted with the vital mission of uniting all the Resistance groups into a single, coordinated organization.

Barbie captured Moulin in 1943 with the help of a French informer. Knowing that Moulin possessed invaluable information about all the Resistance networks, Barbie subjected him to unspeakable tortures over the course of many days and nights. Moulin gave nothing away and finally died in agony with his lips still sealed.

In 1983 the long hunt for Barbie ended when he was arrested by the authorities in Bolivia, South America. They turned the aging Nazi over to the French. He had already been tried and convicted of war crimes *in absentia* (while undercover in South America). Now the French were determined to try him again, on new charges.

Barbie threatened to turn the trial into an exposé of the numerous French citizens—supposedly including persons of high rank—who had collaborated with him in his campaigns against the Resistance. The French investigators proceeded carefully and cautiously. They did not bring Barbie to trial until 1987. Testimony about the collaborationists was judged to be irrelevant and was excluded.

At the trial, Barbie showed that he had lost none of his former arrogance. He scornfully refused to attend most of the trial sessions. He was, however, compelled to hear the harrowing testimony of several survivors of his torture chambers. They identified him as the cool, smiling officer who had personally supervised their ordeals. Barbie was convicted for the second time and sentenced to life imprisonment (France had abolished the death penalty some years earlier).

Despite its tragic losses to men like Barbie, the Resistance scored many victories as well. Its saboteurs blew up an entire aircraft factory in southern France that was making propellers for the Luftwaffe, the German air force. Another group "persuaded" Rudolphe Peugeot, owner of a big French auto-making company, to help them plan and carry out the destruction of his own factories. The Peugeot plants were making tank turrets and aircraft-engine parts for the Germans.

In September 1942, five Resistance men blew up the German navy radio transmitter on the French coast. For weeks after that, the Navy High Command was unable to contact its submarines scattered throughout the Atlantic.

The largest networks in the Resistance, and probably the most active, were those run by the Communist Party. Knowing that they were prime targets of the Gestapo, facing especially merciless treatment if captured, the well-disciplined communists carried on a no-quarter-asked campaign that produced some of the war's most daring exploits.

Many of the Resistance networks focused on gathering intelligence about the German forces. They transmitted the information either to the British or to de Gaulle's Free French headquarters in London.

The most successful of the intelligence networks was known as Alliance. It was headed by Marie-Madeleine Fourcade, one of the many courageous women in the Resistance. By the time the war was over she commanded a network of 3,000 agents throughout France. They supplied a wealth of useful data about the German defense system in Normandy, where the Allies planned to invade in June 1944.

As soon as the Allies did land in Normandy, the Germans ordered one of their most formidable armored divisions to get to that front as fast as possible. This elite outfit was the second SS Panzer Division, called "Das Reich." It had been stationed in southeast France. With its 20,000 men, its hundreds of tanks and self-propelled guns, it could do severe damage to the Allied troops. The trip should have taken the

RETURN FROM EXILE. *General Charles de Gaulle, commander of Free French forces, acknowledges the cheers of Parisians rejoicing over the liberation of their city in August 1944.* Courtesy of *Paris Match*

Le jour de gloire est arrivé

L'apothéose :
le général De Gaulle, follement
acclamé par des milliers
de Parisiens, descend les Champs-Elysées
vers Notre-Dame
pour le Te Deum de
la Libération.

division about three days.

Word went out immediately to the Resistance: Keep Das Reich from reaching Normandy as long as possible. All along the way, at every crossroads, every bridge, every patch of woods, Resistance fighters sprang their ambushes. Each group did its best to disable a few tanks, knock out or even capture some cannon, kill and wound some SS men. Then, in the face of superior German firepower, they faded away into the countryside. To make things worse for Das Reich, the Resistance kept London informed of the Germans' every move. The result was that they were constantly being bombed and strafed by Allied planes.

The Das Reich commanders were livid with fury and frustration. Unable to wipe out the Resistance men swarming around them like killer bees, they decided to take it out on peaceful citizens. In the small town of Tulle, they gathered ninety-nine men and women and hanged them all in the public square.

Then, on June 10, 1944, Das Reich came to the little village of Oradour-sur-Glane. The fact that its people had little connection with the Resistance made no difference. The SS men rounded up all 200 of the village's men and machine-gunned them. Next, 241 women and 202 children were locked in the village church, which was set afire. Anyone trying to get out was shot. Every house in the village was then burned to the ground.

Miraculously, five badly wounded men, one woman who had been hit by five bullets, and one child survived to tell Oradour's tragic story. The ruins of the village have deliberately been left exactly as they remained on that terrible day. One sign at the entrance to the village tells in French how its people were "savagely murdered." Another sign is in German: *Nicht Vergessen* ("Don't Forget"). Visitors from every country pay homage to this French national shrine.

In the early days of the war, in 1940, there were probably no more than 1,000 individuals in the Resistance. It looked very much as if the

Germans would win the war, and a majority of the French chose to stay out of trouble till the fighting ended.

Then the fortunes of war shifted in favor of the Allies. The Resistance began to swell. By January 1944 there were 50,000 in its ranks. By July, after the Allied invasion, it numbered 200,000. Some of these last-minute volunteers had probably been collaborating with the enemy until they hastily switched to the winning side. After the war, thousands of collaborators were exposed, arrested, tried, and punished as traitors.

The Nazis themselves contributed unwittingly to the growth of the Resistance. In 1943 they persuaded the French government to cooperate with them in setting up a Compulsory Labor Force. It was to draft 350,000 young Frenchmen for work in Germany. Instead, thousands of them disappeared into the hills and forests, where almost all joined the Resistance. They came to be known as the *maquis*, because in their toughness and endurance they resembled the scrubby underbrush or *maquis* of the mountain areas where they had their camps. The *maquis* soon acquired a fearsome reputation among the Germans, carrying out many raids and attacks on the occupation forces.

Money for the Resistance's far-flung activities was always a problem. The solution? Steal it! In one daring robbery, Resistants got away with a billion and a half francs (about $200,100,000 at prewar rates) from a Bank of France armored car. Even more spectacular was a train robbery that netted double that amount.

But the greatest prize sought by the Resistance was Paris itself. The Resistance leaders refused to wait for the approaching Allied armies to free the city. They insisted that the capital of France must be freed by French fighting men and women.

In mid-August 1944 the 20,000 fighters of the Paris Resistance launched their assault. They swiftly captured many of the government buildings in the center of the city. For a long and desperate week they held out against everything the Germans could throw at them. By the time the Allies arrived, the Resistance had taken 11,000 German prisoners, killed 2,788, and wounded 4,911. The French had lost far fewer: 901 dead and 1,455 wounded, with 585 civilians killed.

The city went wild with joy when General de Gaulle led the leaders of the Resistance and the provisional government in a triumphant parade down the Champs-Élysées.

U.S. General (later President) Dwight D. Eisenhower was supreme commander of the Allied forces. He wrote in his memoirs after the war that the Resistance had done the work of fifteen regular army divisions. It had shortened the war by at least two months.

U.S. Army Chief of Staff General George C. Marshall expressed the appreciation of every Allied soldier who fought his way from Normandy across France to final victory:

The Resistance surpassed all our expectations, and it was they who, in delaying the arrival of German reinforcements and in preventing the regrouping of enemy divisions . . . assured the success of our landings.

The feelings of the Resistance fighters were expressed simply but eloquently by Albert Camus. A leader of the "Combat" Resistance group, he later became one of France's most renowned authors and a winner of the Nobel Prize for Literature. "What else could we have done?" Camus wrote. "We could *not* be on the side of the concentration camps!" Sadly, as we have seen, some French citizens did choose "the side of the concentration camps." They paid a grim price when the war was over.

The saga of the French Resistance forms only one episode in the long history of this fascinating nation. The people of France have lived through many historic dramas, some ending in glory, some in tragedy. In the course of centuries the people have changed and developed in many ways. At the same time they have never ceased to transform and improve the diverse, beautiful land they live in.

A Nation
of Many Nations

No nation in Europe can claim more ancient or more complex origins than the French. The area that is now France has been invaded by many peoples over the centuries. Some stayed only briefly, while others settled permanently. All left hereditary traces in the French people of today. The invaders have included Ligurians, Iberians, Celts (later called Gauls), Basques, Greeks, Romans, Britons, Frankish tribes from what is now Germany, Northmen from the Scandinavian lands, and Arabs from North Africa.

During the past century and a half France has further enriched its population by opening its gates to more than 4 million immigrants. A majority came from nearby countries such as Spain, Portugal, and Italy. Other Europeans came from the east, especially from Poland.

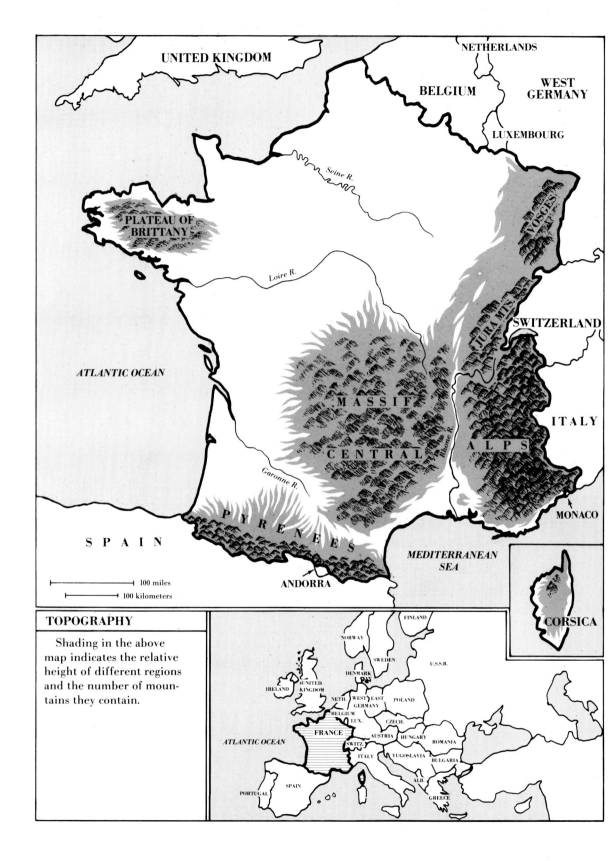

UNITED KINGDOM

NETHERLANDS

BELGIUM

WEST GERMANY

LUXEMBOURG

Seine R.

PLATEAU OF BRITTANY

VOSGES MTS.

Loire R.

JURA MTS.

SWITZERLAND

ATLANTIC OCEAN

M A S S I F

C E N T R A L

Rhône R.

A L P S

ITALY

Garonne R.

MONACO

P Y R E N E E S

S P A I N

MEDITERRANEAN SEA

ANDORRA

100 miles

100 kilometers

CORSICA

TOPOGRAPHY

Shading in the above map indicates the relative height of different regions and the number of mountains they contain.

FINLAND

NORWAY

SWEDEN

DENMARK

IRELAND

UNITED KINGDOM

NETH.

WEST GERMANY

EAST GERMANY

POLAND

U.S.S.R.

BELGIUM

LUX.

CZECH.

ATLANTIC OCEAN

FRANCE

SWITZ.

AUSTRIA

HUNGARY

ROMANIA

ITALY

YUGOSLAVIA

BULGARIA

PORTUGAL

SPAIN

ALB.

GREECE

More recently, France's former colonies have sent throngs of newcomers. From North Africa have come mostly Arabs, giving France the largest such population by far of any country in Europe. Immigrants from the former French possessions in west and central Africa and from West Indian islands still ruled by France have been largely black.

Still another racial element has been added to the mix by refugees from the one-time French colonies of Vietnam and other parts of Indochina. About 120,000 have settled in France since the end of the Vietnam war in 1975, joining the thousands of Asians already there. France increasingly resembles the United States in this respect: It has become a multiracial society.

The French Character

Can a people of such diverse origins have developed a unique and recognizable national character? Some experts believe that the French have.

A book called *I'm Going to France,* published in 1986 by a French government agency for foreigners planning to study in France, describes one set of personality traits said to form part of the French character.

The French, says this publication, "remain very much attached to liberal traditions . . . they reject all forms of constraint . . . [and] they submit themselves to any form of discipline with difficulty." The book notes further that French men and women are "quick to criticize . . . and to assert their rights." Moreover, they "do not hesitate to question their own institutions and to demonstrate, even in the presence of outsiders, a remarkable lack of respect for established authority."

The book adds a word of caution for foreigners: the French "prefer that the criticism should come from themselves . . . they do not always appreciate it when the criticism comes from others."

"On the whole," the book concludes, the people of France tend to be "tolerant . . . and respectful of the opinions and beliefs of others, even if they do not share them." They got their subtle way of thinking from the Greeks, their logical way of doing things from the Germans, their tendency toward fantasy from the Celts.

On the subject of tolerance, the brilliant sixteenth-century French essayist Michel de Montaigne put forth his personal attitude as a model for his countrymen:

I look upon all men as my compatriots, and embrace a Pole as a Frenchman, making less account of the national than of the universal and common bond.

A noble ideal, certainly, but one that few nations have been able to fulfill consistently and completely. At various times in their history the French have demonstrated their tolerance by opening up their country as a place of asylum for the oppressed, the persecuted, the impoverished. At other times they have themselves been the oppressors and the persecutors. There is no one simple way to sum up their national character. As much as most other nations, perhaps more than some, they are a people of complexities and contradictions.

The contradictions in the French character have also been described by Alain Peyrefitte, a senator in the French Parliament, former Cabinet officer, and member of the French Academy:

capable of gallantry but unruly; enthusiastic but disorganized. Men of dazzling exploits rather than . . . tenacity, of individual prowess rather than of collective discipline . . . sparkling at one moment, obstinate the next, by turns heroic and panicky, always finding it difficult to live together. . . .

A surprisingly critical opinion was expressed by Charles de Gaulle, who led the Free French in World War II and later served as president of France. Commenting on French political attitudes in 1966, de Gaulle said that the French "cannot do without the State and yet they detest it, except when there is danger. . . . They do not behave like adults."

Yet the French character is also capable of drastic change. Foreigners visiting France in the first two decades after World War II often encountered a French tendency to be touchy, inhospitable, sometimes arrogant. But those were years when the country had barely begun to overcome the embittering effects of a humiliating military defeat, four years of harsh German occupation, and seemingly endless bombings and battles that ravaged the country. Large parts of the population had lost their homes. Many were living in crowded and uncomfortable conditions. Could any nation be expected to invite guests to their homes or to be smiling and friendly under such circumstances?

Visitors to France in recent years report a decidedly different experience. With their country now largely rebuilt, with their economy developing at a swift pace, with high technology everywhere replacing outmoded ways of living and working, the French these days are more relaxed, more confident, more genial.

In the old days, the average Frenchman might invite a special foreign guest for drinks at a local café, or for dinner at a good restaurant. He would almost never invite the guest to his home. Postwar homes were likely to be embarrassingly shabby. Today, French homes are as open to invited guests as those in any land.

But there are probably as many ideas about the French character as there are individuals who have ever had anything to do with this charming, highly intelligent, often unpredictable people.

The Immigrant Dilemma

Does French tolerance toward others extend to the immigrants? The answer is mixed. Few facts of modern life arouse stronger and more varied reactions among the French than the influx of immigrants. The immigrants constitute nearly 9 percent of the wage earners, though they form only about 7 percent of the population. But they also suffer from higher rates of unemployment than the French.

Most immigrants do unskilled or semiskilled work in such fields as construction, automobile assembly, textile manufacturing, and health. They have higher on-the-job accident rates, because the jobs available to them are often risky.

An estimated 300,000 to 500,000 immigrants are unable to obtain papers entitling them to live and work in France legally. These illegals tend to be the most brutally exploited at work—sometimes by employers from their own countries.

Immigrant workers make a contribution to the French economy that would be hard to replace. Their generally low wages are believed to be a major factor in keeping French products competitive in the world market. The largest part of their wages is spent in France, though a portion may be sent to families in their homelands. They also pay substantial taxes.

French attitudes toward the immigrants have become less friendly since the country encountered serious economic problems in the 1970s and 1980s. A steep increase in unemployment has been the chief cause of rising hostility. Large sections of the public are convinced that the immigrants take jobs away from French citizens. In fact, most jobs taken by immigrants involve menial and sometimes dangerous work that the French tend to avoid.

Illegal immigrants are especially resented. Government policy toward them has shifted. In the mid-1970s the government offered grants of F 10,000 ($1,666) to immigrants willing to return to their native lands. Many did so between 1977 and 1979, but the number going home has shrunk to a mere 1,000 a year since then.

Right after the elections of 1981, newly elected President François Mitterrand announced a program designed to clean up the situation by granting legal status to some 130,000 illegals. The unexpected result was to bring in a new wave of almost twice as many more undocumented immigrants.

A public opinion poll taken by the popular *Paris-Match* magazine showed that 86 percent of the French public think all illegals should be driven out of the country. Mitterrand's Socialist government denounced this attitude as racist and took little action against the illegals.

Immigration has declined sharply in recent years. The foreign population was growing at a rate of 4.5 percent annually in the early 1970s. Today the rate is around 0.7 percent.

The figures on immigration contrast dramatically with those on emigration from France. Through all the centuries of French history, the number who have left their homeland permanently has been relatively insignificant. Small groups of descendants of French emigrants can be found today in eastern Canada, in Louisiana, in areas of the Caribbean governed by France (Martinique, Guadeloupe, French Guiana), and in the former French colonies in Asia and Africa.

Large numbers of French citizens do go abroad to live and to work for varying periods of time. There are currently about a million and a half of these. Most work for private companies, while many others serve in education or other forms of public employment. The vast majority live in other European countries, with perhaps half as many in Africa and smaller numbers in the Americas or the Pacific area. But virtually all look forward to going home someday and to living out their days in their beloved native land.

Prejudice— And Those Who Fight It

The most easily accepted and assimilated immigrants are nearly a million Portuguese, half a million Italians, and an approximately equal number of Spaniards. Most share the religion of France's Roman Catholic majority. Their native languages are also similar enough to French to make learning that language relatively easy.

Attitudes toward the Arab immigrants from North Africa are less welcoming. Their Islamic religion is alien to the French. Because they are generally darker-skinned as well, they face a special form of racial prejudice—despite the fact that Arabs are actually members of the Caucasian or "white" race.

Contributing further to the widespread resentment against them are the bitter memories of the eight-year Algerian war (1954–1962). The French made a heavy investment of blood and treasure in the futile struggle to keep Algeria French. When the decision was finally forced upon them to give Algeria its independence, about a million and a half French settlers had to abandon their properties in Algeria and resettle in France. These people, along with many other French patriots, have never forgiven the Arabs for this humiliation.

A number of additional factors keep the Arab immigrants apart from the general population. For many years most Arabs could find housing only in shantytowns on the fringes of towns and cities. Today they live mostly in low-cost government-subsidized housing developments built in the last thirty years. But wherever they live, they are almost always segregated.

Many of them persist in speaking Arabic among themselves. Some tend to dress in ways different from the French. They generally prefer the fragrant, spicy foods of their homelands.

Like minorities in the United States, the Arabs tend to be blamed for many of France's social problems: unemployment, rising crime rates, rising welfare and education costs. In 1983 the French government's Ministry for Immigration Affairs prepared a booklet refuting these charges. It showed that unemployment had risen after 1975, precisely when immigration leveled off. Crime rates were no higher among the Arabs than among native-born Frenchmen of the same class. With so many of them at work or actively seeking it, the Arabs constituted no unusual drain on welfare. And since most of them arrived as young adults, they saved France the cost of educating them.

About 22 million copies of this booklet were printed. For reasons that have never been made clear, they were withdrawn from circulation and have not been distributed to the public.

It is a fact that the crime rate has been rising. In the mid-1970s it stood at about forty crimes per 1,000 inhabitants. It has since risen to about fifty-eight. The increase is reportedly due mostly to petty crimes. No connection between immigration and crime rates has ever been shown. The French crime rate is considerably lower than the American.

Oddly, there is less prejudice against blacks. One reason is probably that they are fewer than the Arabs in France. Another reason may be that a majority of the black immigrants are middle class and well educated. Most Arabs are working class and have less education.

A very different form of prejudice, anti-Semitism, has a long history in France. The approximately 700,000 Jews in France form the largest Jewish community in Europe outside Russia. Until World War II they were predominantly Ashkenazic Jews from Eastern Europe. Today the majority are Sephardic Jews from Spain and North Africa. While many have achieved success in business and the professions, they are subject to varied forms of social and economic discrimination.

French anti-Semitism can be traced at least as far back as the persecution of Jews during the Middle Ages. But the best-known historical example is the case of Captain Alfred Dreyfus. He was one of the few Jewish officers in the French army. Accused of selling military secrets to the Germans in 1894, he was convicted by a rigged court-martial and condemned to solitary confinement for life on Devil's Island. For twelve years the nation was almost torn apart by bitter controversy between his supporters and his enemies. Dreyfus was fully cleared in 1906 and restored to his position in the army.

World War II saw a revival of anti-Semitic prejudice. The French government passed anti-Jewish laws that went beyond even those that the Hitler government had passed against the Jews of Germany. It collaborated with the Germans in deporting 117,000 French Jews to the

HOPEFUL NEWCOMER. *A North African immigrant looking for work arrives in Marseilles. His chances of gaining admission to France will depend partly on his answers to the questions on the document he is holding.* ILO/Photo by J. Mohr/Distributed by U.N.

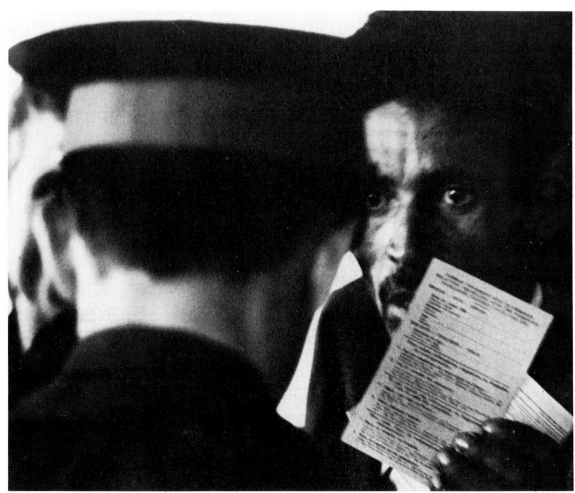

Nazi death camps. Though men and women of the Resistance rescued some, the general population did little to help. Some even took advantage of the situation and profited from the Jews' expulsion.

Yet there is a powerful current of public opinion that opposes mistreatment of Jews—especially when it takes the form of violence. In 1976 a memorial honoring the Jewish victims of the Holocaust was erected at Draney, outside Paris, site of the camp from which they were deported. Then in October 1980 a bomb exploded outside a synagogue in Paris, killing four people. It was apparently set by an Arab terrorist group. The response was one of the biggest demonstrations France has ever seen. Thousands of people, of all races, religions, and political parties, marched down the Champs-Élysées to protest the attack.

Politics provides another revealing example of French ambivalence about Jews. The country has had two Jewish prime ministers in the twentieth century, Léon Blum and Pierre Mendès-France.

In recent years France has witnessed a disturbing growth of neofascist movements. Racism—aimed primarily against the Arab minority but against other groups as well—is a basic theme of their propaganda. One such movement, the National Front, has won as much as 14.4 percent of the vote in elections of the 1980s. The Front's platform is to "free France" of "nonwhite" workers who are supposedly taking Frenchmen's jobs.

In the fall of 1984, a small group of friends formed a new organization they named SOS Racism. It is dedicated to challenging and changing racist attitudes in France. Its leader, who bears the fascinating name Harlem Désir, is the son of French and West Indian parents. The group's membership has grown rapidly, particularly among those in their twenties and thirties. By mid-1988 it had 15,000 members in France and affiliated groups in Belgium, Sweden, Switzerland, Norway,

and Canada. Its catchy slogan, *Touche pas à mon pote!* ("Hands off my buddy!"), appeared on buttons, T-shirts, and posters all over France.

In March 1985 a young Moroccan was killed by two Frenchmen who were outraged when they saw him talking to a white woman. Not long afterward, a bomb exploded at a Jewish film festival in Paris. SOS Racism organized a giant rally of over 300,000 "buddies" at the famous Place de la Concorde in the center of Paris. One notable feature was that Jews and Arabs marched together.

In 1988, when SOS launched a national "Week of Education" to bring its message to schools across the country, President François Mitterrand visited a classroom to kick off the campaign.

Whatever their present problems, the French remain a proud people. Their long and distinguished history, their struggles to establish and maintain themselves as a unified nation, their far-famed contributions to world science and culture abundantly justify their pride.

Today their unity sometimes appears to be endangered by friction among the diverse elements that make up their population. But there are signs that out of these difficulties the French are forging a new and stronger unity.

FIGHTER AGAINST HATRED. *Harlem Désir is the founder and leader of* SOS Racisme, *a French group that fights prejudice and discrimination against minorities. The poster behind him bears the group's slogan: "Hands Off My Buddy!"* Agence France Presse/ Kovarik

CHAPTER III

The Shaping
of the French
Nation

The history of France is a history of age-old traditions—and rapid, often revolutionary changes. It is a history of generosity and tolerance—and of violence and persecutions. It is the tumultuous history of a great nation constantly in the process of becoming.

Prehistoric Traces

The land that is now called France has been inhabited since remote prehistoric times. Modern archeologists have traced the first signs of human activity to more than 750,000 years ago. The apelike creatures of that era could make only the most primitive tools and weapons, by striking or chipping one stone against another.

Much later, about 10,000 to 20,000 years ago, a more advanced race occupied an area around the Dordogne River, in southwestern France. Now called the Cro-Magnon tribes, they are believed to have migrated from Asia, perhaps along the shores of the Mediterranean Sea. They were taller than their predecessors. Their well-shaped heads contained brains as large as those of present-day humans. Their tools were made with considerable skill.

Remarkable Cro-Magnon accomplishments were the paintings on their cave walls. They drew amazingly lifelike reindeer, bison, horses, and cattle, in colors that have lasted for 20,000 years. The paintings probably served religious or magical purposes, to ensure the success of the hunt. The largest of the caves containing them were open to the public for many years, but recently they were closed in order to protect

20,000-YEAR-OLD MASTERPIECES. *The highly skilled artists who painted these graceful and lifelike animals on cave walls were prehistoric hunters, who once lived in southwestern France.* The Bettmann Archive

the paintings. Precise copies can be seen in artificial caves specially built nearby, close to the town of Lascaux in southwestern France.

Still more recently, about 8,000 years ago, another prehistoric tribe left impressive stone monuments in the northwestern area now called Brittany. Some of these giant stones, called *menhirs*, stand erect to heights of up to 21.2 meters (70 feet). The menhirs are arranged in wide circles called *cromlechs*. Atop many are great flat stones known as *dolmens*. The purpose of these strange groupings is still something of a mystery. They may have been memorials for the dead; or they may have served as some sort of lunar calendar.

Celts and Gauls

The first tribes to invade and conquer large areas of northern Europe in historic times were the Celts. These stockily built, rather dark-skinned warriors probably came from the Danube regions of eastern Europe about 1,000 B.C. They may have originated in Asia long before.

The Celtic tribes were never united. They had no written language. Traces of their spoken tongue persist in French and to a greater extent in the languages spoken by other west European peoples of Celtic origin, such as the Irish and the Welsh. Some 450 ancient Celtic words are still known. Modern French uses fewer than thirty.

Those Celts who settled in the area that is France today came to be called Gauls. They had a well-developed social system ruled by aristocrats. Slaves captured in battle did much of the necessary labor. The Celts' largest settlements were called *oppida*, which were hardly more than enclosed camps built on high ground.

CELTIC SCULPTURE. *This low-relief stone carving was executed by a Celtic craftsman, in the Roman province of Gaul, between the first and fourth centuries* A.D. Courtesy of French Embassy, Press and Information Division

One of the oppida later grew into the city of a Gallic tribe called the Parisii. Called Lutetia, it stood on the site of present-day Paris.

Greek and Roman Gaul

A significant new influence entered Gaul around 600 B.C. Greek colonists founded a port they called Massilia, on the Mediterranean coast. This is the origin of the bustling modern city of Marseilles. As trade grew between the Gauls and the Greeks, the highly developed civilization of Greece introduced the Gauls to new ways of life.

From time to time Massilia was threatened by barbarian marauders. The Greek colonists were unable to get much help from their own country. Around 154 B.C. they invited the rising new Mediterranean power, Rome, to help repel the barbarians. The Romans were only too pleased to enter Gaul, for it formed a useful land bridge to their own colony of Hispania, now known as Spain.

A dynamic new general assumed command of the Roman forces in Gaul in 59 B.C. His name was Julius Caesar. His first task was to drive out two invading forces, the Germans and the Helvetii. Then he turned his attention to the Gauls themselves.

In a long and well-planned campaign, Caesar smashed the Gallic tribes and captured their chief, Vercingetorix. Caesar paraded the defeated warrior through Rome in a great triumphal procession and eventually had him put to death. Oddly, a fictional Gallic chieftain named Astérix became the hero of the most popular series of comic books of the early 1980s.

Caesar's conquest of Gaul was so ruthless and complete that Rome

ROMAN REMAINS. *The 2,000-year-old arena and amphitheater at Arles demonstrate the skill of their Roman builders. The arena is still used for the annual Festival of Music and Drama and other events.* Courtesy of French Embassy, Press and Information Division

was able to rule the province for the next 500 years. To ensure the Gauls' submission and loyalty, many were awarded citizenship in the Roman empire. The Roman religion replaced that of Gaul.

The Romans further strengthened their control by building an excellent network of military roads. Towns and cities began to develop along these highways. The capital of Roman Gaul was Lugdunum, now called Lyons.

In one of their most lasting contributions, the Romans taught their language—Latin—to all the tribes. Latin eventually developed into the family of modern languages known as the Romance languages. These include French, Spanish, Portuguese, Italian, and Rumanian.

The Middle Ages

By the fifth century A.D. the rulers of the Roman Empire had become so corrupt, and their once-invincible legions had become so unreliable, that they could no longer defend their vast territories. Germanic tribes known as the Goths and the Vandals broke through to the heart of the empire and sacked the city of Rome. In A.D. 476 these barbarian invaders deposed the last western Roman emperor—signaling the fall of the Roman Empire.

There also existed an eastern empire, with its capital at Constantinople. Its ruler now claimed jurisdiction over all Christendom.

Without the protection of the Roman legions, Gaul was overrun first by Asian aggressors called Huns, and then by another Germanic tribe, the Franks. The Frankish king, Clovis, occupied Paris in A.D. 486.

A pagan at the time of his victory, Clovis married a Christian princess and was converted to Christianity. These acts ensured him of the powerful backing of the Church in his struggle to eliminate several rivals for the throne. Once secure in power, he established a dynasty that has come to be known as the Merovingians.

Clovis upheld a concept of kingship that was to exert a varying influence down through the centuries. He believed that the king's power was absolute and that this power could be inherited by the king's male heirs. This tradition prevailed while the Merovingians ruled France for about 300 years. They ruled under principles that allowed local aristocrats to exercise a share of power.

In the seventh century a palace official named Pépin overthrew the Merovingians and established a new dynasty, the Carolingians.

Pépin's son Charlemagne made himself into one of the most power-

Important Kings and Their Reigns (481–1792)

DYNASTIES	KINGS
Merovingian (481–751)	Clovis (481–511)
Carolingian (751–987)	Charlemagne (768–814)
Capetian (987–1589)	Hugh Capet (987–996)
	Philip Augustus (1180–1223)
	Louis IX (St. Louis) (1226–1270)
	Francis I (1515–1547)
Bourbon (1589–1792)	Henry IV (1589–1610)
	Louis XIII (1610–1643)
	Louis XIV (1643–1715)
	Louis XV (1715–1774)
	Louis XVI (1774–1792)

ful rulers in all history. A formidable personality and an immensely skilled warrior chieftain, he conducted over fifty victorious military campaigns. Ultimately he conquered almost all of western Europe.

One of the few setbacks Charlemagne encountered occurred during a campaign against the Saracens in Spain. It gave rise to a durable legend, embodied in the most famous of the medieval epic poems called the *chansons de geste* (''songs of heroic deeds''). This one is called *La Chanson de Roland* (*The Song of Roland*).

The historical reality underlying the poem is that Charlemagne was besieging the powerful fortress of Saragossa. When he heard that a major revolt had broken out on the northern borders of his empire, he withdrew his armies to meet the new challenge. As the troops passed through the dangerous Pyrenees mountains, the army's rear was protected by a small force under the command of a young duke named Roland. Without warning, Roland's men were attacked by hordes of Basque warriors in a narrow valley called Roncesvalles. The Frankish warriors fought gallantly but were overwhelmed by superior numbers and wiped out.

In the long view of history this was actually a minor battle of no lasting significance, but over the next two centuries it was blown up into a colorful tale of unparalleled courage and heroism. In the poem Roland's companion Oliver, seeing them totally outnumbered, urges Roland to call back the Emperor and the army with a blast upon his mighty horn. Roland's disdainful reply provides a fine sample of the poem's high-flown romantic style:

> . . . May never God allow
> That I should bring dishonor on my house
> Or on fair France bring any ill renown!
> Rather will I with Durendal [his sword] strike out,
> With this good sword, here on my baldrick [belt] bound;
> From point to hilt you'll see the blood run down. . . .

The anonymous authors of the poem depict Roland and his dauntless companions as killing incredible numbers of the enemy before they are themselves struck down. Their death is fittingly avenged as Charlemagne has the evil duke who was responsible for Roland's ambush executed.

In real life, Charlemagne established a system of government that later became the foundation for feudalism, a form of social organization that prevailed throughout Europe for almost 1,000 years. Charlemagne's system was based on two principles: (1) All free citizens of the kingdom must swear a personal and direct oath of loyalty to him; (2) the common people must bind themselves as "vassals" to a nobleman or overlord. That meant that they owed the noble their allegiance and a portion of their crops. In return, the noble owed them his armed protection. The nobles, in turn, were vassals of the king.

Charlemagne's prefeudal system worked well as long as it was headed by so revered a monarch as he was. It had the dangerous weakness, however, that it depended too heavily on one man to outlast his death. The feudal system that eventually took its place was much more decentralized.

A profoundly religious man, Charlemagne was dismayed by the ignorance and illiteracy of his people and of many of the priests. He assembled the wise and learned men of the realm at his court, turning it into a kind of palace academy. He encouraged them to preserve the accumulated knowledge of Europe's scholars and to develop it further.

Charlemagne also believed that the people must be educated to a proper understanding of the Scriptures. In 789 he decreed that a school must be established in every monastery and at the seat of every bishop. The children would be taught by the priests, with payment to be entirely voluntary.

In 800 Pope Leo III asked Charlemagne to come to Rome to assist him in dealing with his enemies. Charlemagne agreed and helped re-

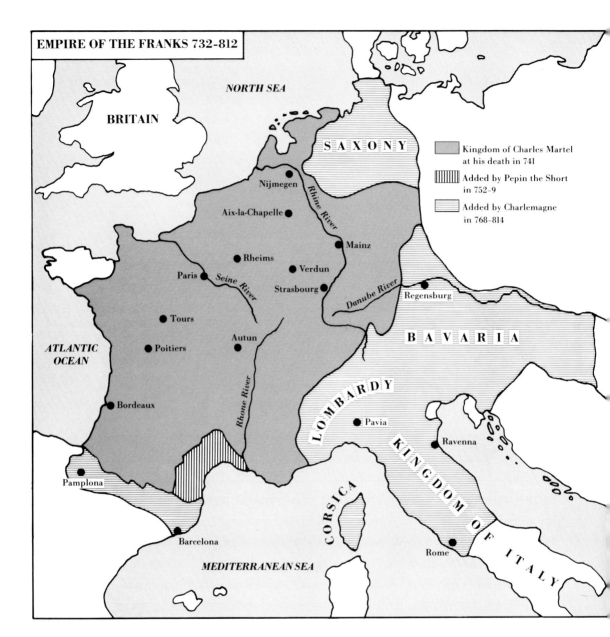

NORTH SEA

BRITAIN

S A X O N Y

Nijmegen

Aix-la-Chapelle

Mainz

Rheims

Paris

Verdun

Strasbourg

Regensburg

Tours

Autun

B A V A R I A

ATLANTIC
OCEAN

Poitiers

Bordeaux

L O M B A R D Y

Pavia

Ravenna

K I N G D O M

O F

I T A L Y

Pamplona

C O R S I C A

Barcelona

Rome

MEDITERRANEAN SEA

Rhine River

Seine River

Danube River

Rhone River

Kingdom of Charles Martel
at his death in 741

Added by Pepin the Short
in 752–9

Added by Charlemagne
in 768–814

solve the Pope's difficulties. On Christmas Day he was attending Mass
when the Pope suddenly placed a golden crown on his head and had
him acclaimed with the ancient title of Holy Roman Emperor.

Actually, this seemingly unexpected action had been planned by

Charlemagne and the Pope. At that moment the throne of the Roman Empire happened to be vacant. Charlemagne felt that he had proved himself the true defender of the faith and merited the title.

After Charlemagne's death, his mighty empire was divided among his heirs. One of them was given authority over the area that included France.

By the year 987 there were no direct legitimate descendants of Charlemagne to claim the throne. The most important French noblemen came together and elected a new king from among themselves. This was a noteworthy change from the hereditary tradition of the Merovingians and Carolingians. It also foreshadowed political developments that lay in the far future.

The new king's name was Hugh Capet. He had formerly ruled the province of Ile de France, the region surrounding Paris.

Hugh Capet had been chosen because he was less wealthy and powerful than the dukes and counts who elected him and hence less of a threat to their power. But his Capetian dynasty gradually extended its power over the entire country and ruled it for 600 years.

At the time of Capet's election, the Atlantic coast of France was prey to raids by Norsemen, the fierce Viking marauders from Scandinavia. Some of them settled in the fertile countryside. Eventually the region was even named after them: Normandy. In the tenth century the king of France yielded it to the Normans permanently.

In 1066 William, Duke of Normandy, laid claim to the English throne. He invaded England and defeated the English forces in a great battle at Hastings, not far from the southeast coast. Soon he had subdued the entire kingdom, earning the title William the Conqueror. He was crowned King of England, while retaining control of Normandy.

The long-range result of William's conquest was 500 years of on-again, off-again war between rival French and English claimants to the

NORMAN CONQUEST. *William, Duke of Normandy, became William the Conqueror after his victory at the Battle of Hastings in 1066. The story is depicted in the multi-paneled Bayeux Tapestry, a seamless embroidery over 200 feet long.* Courtesy of French Embassy, Press and Information Division

two countries' thrones. The English kings kept putting forth the claim that their descent from William gave them the right to rule large areas in France.

By the thirteenth century, the English had conquered several provinces in western and central France. French King Louis IX won back some of these territories and made peace with the English. An immensely popular ruler, he is vividly enshrined in the French mind as seated under an old oak tree at Vincennes, dispensing justice impartially to the humblest and the wealthiest of his subjects. One of the most pious rulers in all French history, he led his armies in two of the Crusades, seeking vainly to free the Holy Land from Muslim rule. He died during one of these expeditions. The Catholic Church later elevated him to sainthood.

Louis IX's reign was notable also for the emergence of a brilliant group of Catholic philosophers and theologians known as Scholastics or Schoolmen. Outstanding among them was Thomas Aquinas (1225?–1274), author of the classic treatise *Summa Theologiae* (*Summary of Theology*) and many other works. The Italian-born Aquinas lived in Paris for about twelve years and did some of his most important work there.

A master of logic, Aquinas reconciled faith with reason and harmonized the teachings of Aristotle with Christian doctrine. His writings remain to this day the basis of Roman Catholic theological teaching.

FIRST CRUSADE. *Godfrey of Bouillon, Duke of lower Lorraine (wearing the crown), leads an assault on the fortress of Jerusalem in 1099. Many French noblemen, including at least one king, took part in subsequent crusades.* Courtesy of French Government Tourist Office

Pope John XXII canonized Aquinas in 1323, and in 1880 the Church declared this great teacher the patron saint of Catholic schools.

Toward the end of the thirteenth century King Philip IV of France became embroiled in a series of disputes with Pope Boniface VIII. At first the issue was money. Needing funds for war with England, the king levied taxes on the French clergy. The Pope denied his right to do this without papal consent. Philip then cut off all payment of revenues from France to the Pope. The latter yielded—temporarily.

Boniface was determined to assert papal authority over all the kings of Europe. Philip absolutely rejected this claim, and relations between them rapidly deteriorated. Boniface died soon afterward.

The year 1305 saw the election of Clement V, a French pope. King Philip persuaded Clement to take the drastic step of moving the Papacy out of Rome to Avignon, in southern France. The city was a papal possession, but Philip felt he could control the Pope better there.

The Papacy remained in Avignon until 1378, under seven popes. Finally it returned to Rome, where, after a confused period in which there were two different lines of popes, it has remained ever since. Avignon remained under papal ownership until 1789, when its people voted to join France.

In 1338 King Edward III of England declared himself king of France. The long struggle that then ensued is known as the Hundred Years' War. It lasted till 1453.

In the early years of the war Europe faced another great calamity of a very different kind. Called the Black Death, it was an epidemic of bubonic plague that raged through much of Europe from 1347 to about 1350. By the time it subsided, it had killed an estimated one third to one half of the population.

The turning point of the war came in 1429. A mystical and patriotic young woman arrived at the French royal court. She was destined to

JOAN OF ARC. *On May 7th and 8th every year, the citizens of Orléans celebrate victory over the British in 1429 by troops under Joan's inspired leadership. Orléans' young women compete for the honor of portraying Joan.*   Courtesy of French Embassy, Press and Information Division

become world-famous as Joan of Arc. Joan had been seeing visions and hearing voices that commanded her to drive out the English. Her victory would open the way for the Dauphin (son of the dead King Charles VI) to be crowned as Charles VII in the great cathedral of Rheims.

At that time the English were besieging the city of Orléans. Joan persuaded the Dauphin to put her in command of a small force. Her presence so inspired the troops that they broke the siege. After winning more victories, Joan saw her dream come true with the coronation of the King.

Joan of Arc was captured during a subsequent battle. The English put her on trial as a heretic and a witch. They condemned her to be burned at the stake. The weak-willed Charles VII did nothing to help her.

A quarter century after her death, a papal court reversed the trial verdict. Nearly 500 years later, the Catholic Church canonized her as Saint Joan. By that time she had become France's national heroine, revered both for her patriotism and for her piety.

The Glory and Decay of Absolute Monarchy

By the fifteenth century, France was the largest unified state in western Europe. Its people lived under a fully developed system of feudalism. This form of social organization entailed mutual obligations among all classes. At the top were the king and the other powerful feudal lords who ruled vast estates known as fiefs. The lower noblemen who governed parts of the estates were vassals. They owed a portion of their crops and military service to the lords who ruled them, and who were obligated to protect them in times of danger.

The actual farming was done by a class of peasants called serfs. They had few rights, lived lives of wretchedness, and could be bought and sold along with the land they lived on.

Renaissance and Reformation

In the early 1500s the brilliant and strong-willed King Francis I imposed his authority on the other nobles. He won recognition of the king's right to exercise supreme power over the entire country. France was ruled by a stronger and more centralized government than had existed even in the days of Charlemagne.

Francis I was also eager to promote the development of culture in France. He was sensitive to the new artistic and intellectual movements that had begun to develop in Italy around 1300, and that spread to the rest of Europe over the next three centuries. These movements have come to be known as the Renaissance.

The French word *renaissance* literally means "rebirth." It denotes the rebirth of interest in worldly realities, in science and nature, in human thought and feeling, and in the classic works of ancient Greece and Rome that swept the Western intellectual and artistic world from about 1300 to 1650. This great cultural flowering was first reflected in the work of French scientists, artists, and writers after 1500.

Perhaps the most typical figure of the French Renaissance was author François Rabelais. Trained in theology, the law, and medicine, he exemplified the passion for knowledge and experience that characterized the era. His joyous writings expressed an earthy love of life in the language of the streets, the open road, and the high seas. His most famous novels are *Pantagruel* (1533) and *Gargantua* (1535).

Underlying Rabelais' superficial tone of fun lay an earnest humanistic intent. Thus in *Pantagruel* he lectures his readers (humorously addressed as "drinkers") on a decidedly serious subject:

And note here, you drinkers, that the proper method of treating and holding a newly conquered country . . . is not by plundering, forcing, tormenting, ruining, and vexing their people. . . .

Like a newborn child, these conquered peoples must be suckled, cradled, and pleased . . . in such a fashion that there will come to be for them no other king or prince in the world whom they would less willingly have as an enemy or one whom they would prefer to have as a friend.

Rabelais has justifiably been called "the first great and truly popular writer of the modern world."

Francis I befriended and assisted the artists, scholars, and poets of his day. He brought the famous Italian genius Leonardo da Vinci to France and supported him in his old age.

During this same period, Europe was torn apart by a religious movement called the Reformation. Churchmen in several countries challenged certain Catholic doctrines and denounced the corrupt practices that had spread among the clergy. The Reformers insisted, for example, that the Church held no exclusive right to interpret the Bible but that the people had the right to read and interpret it for themselves. The Reformation eventually grew into a worldwide movement that split the Church, caused a series of bitter wars, and gave rise to Protestantism.

One of the most important leaders of the Reformation was a French priest, John Calvin. His efforts had begun to produce a Protestant following in France when he was forced to go into exile in Switzerland. French Protestants were called Huguenots.

By the 1560s there were about 2,000 Huguenot churches in France. But the spread of Protestantism produced a fierce reaction among the Catholic majority. Persecution of the Huguenots climaxed in the massacre of thousands on Saint Bartholomew's Day, 1572. Civil wars between Catholics and Protestants raged intermittently for thirty years.

The strife ended with the coronation of King Henry IV in 1594. Born a Protestant, he knew that he could never gain the throne or end the fighting unless he converted. Saying "Paris is well worth a Mass," he became a Catholic, was crowned king, and was at last permitted to enter

"PARIS IS WELL WORTH A MASS." *King Henry IV enters Paris to claim his throne, after abandoning his Protestant faith and converting to Catholicism.* Courtesy of French Embassy, Press and Information Division

Paris and take control of the kingdom.

One of Henry's first acts as king was to approve the Edict of Nantes. This historic proclamation granted equal political rights and freedom of conscience to Protestants. They could now practice their religion openly, though only in certain parts of the country.

Absolute Monarchy

Henry IV was the first of five Bourbon kings who ruled France for the next 200 years. He regarded the old feudal system as outmoded and inefficient because it kept the country divided. Henry bribed many of the feudal lords to turn over control of their provinces to him. He built highways and canals to knit the country together. He founded the silk industry in France, established the famous Gobelin tapestry workshops, and ordered the construction of one of Paris's most beautiful bridges, the Pont Neuf (New Bridge).

This tolerant and extremely popular king was assassinated by a religious fanatic in 1610.

Henry's son Louis succeeded to the throne. Louis XIII was the first king to turn over a considerable share of power to a chief minister, who helped set policy and run the government. The man chosen for this appointment was the brilliant Cardinal Richelieu.

Louis and Richelieu agreed on the goal of further strengthening the king's power over the feudal aristocrats. In the field of foreign policy, Richelieu expanded French influence in Europe and backed private companies that were establishing French colonies in Asia, Africa, the West Indies, and America.

Richelieu was transformed into a figure of evil in one of the most popular historical adventure novels ever written, *The Three Musketeers*, by the elder Alexandre Dumas. The cardinal is portrayed as a power-hungry tyrant, dominating the timid Louis XIII and plotting against unhappy Queen Anne.

His scheming is frustrated by the fearless but naive young swordsman d'Artagnan. He is mightily sustained by his three indomitable comrades in the regiment of the king's musketeers, the laconic Athos, the gallant Porthos, and the pious Aramis. Their ringing slogan has become familiar to young and old around the world: "All for one, one for all!"

Both Louis XIII and Richelieu died in the early 1640s. The king's son, heir to the throne, was only five years old. Richelieu's successor, Cardinal Mazarin, governed the country until the young prince grew up. He continued Richelieu's policies.

France had earlier become involved in long wars with the Hapsburg Empire and Spain. Victory came in 1648, and Mazarin negotiated the Treaties of Westphalia so skillfully that France gained considerable territory.

Louis XIV was twenty-three years old when Mazarin died in 1661. He had never dared to challenge the cardinal. Now he took over the government and proceeded to rule alone, without any chief minister. Only a limited share of power was allowed to the able comptroller-general of finances, Jean Baptiste Colbert.

Believing in an active economic role for the State, Colbert promoted manufacturing and commerce, built up the navy, and developed the French colonies overseas.

Louis XIV eventually concentrated so much authority in his own hands that he became the most powerful absolute monarch western Europe had ever seen. He believed deeply in the ancient idea that kings ruled by "divine right." He became known as the Sun King, and the symbol of a radiant sun bearing his initial, *L,* appeared on many public buildings.

One manifestation of his power was construction of the immense, extravagant Palace of Versailles. It was no mere showplace. Louis used it as a center of power, compelling all the important nobles to live there under his control. He and he alone decided which individuals should benefit from augmented revenues, advantageous marriages, major military commands, or other signs of royal favor. The slightest sign of his disapproval could mean disaster.

The king insisted that his courtiers maintain a costly and elaborate life-style, with large retinues of servants, stables of horses, and gilded carriages. Even their everyday clothing had to be lavish. When attend-

SUN KING. *King Louis XIV, shown in full regalia, is idealized in this portrait as the protector of the arts.* Courtesy of French Embassy, Press and Information Division

ing the constant round of balls, banquets, and other gala festivals, they competed with each other in sheer extravagance and in the hope of pleasing the king. All this was no mere whim of his. The expense of court life kept the nobles in financial need—and thus dependent on the royal favor.

The daily rituals of the court were intricate and, for ambitious nobles, obligatory. The day started with the king's awakening at eight o'clock. First the queen and the children, then the court officials and most important nobles were admitted to the king's chamber as he dressed and breakfasted, all according to a rigid, prescribed order. At lunch and dinner there were invariably large numbers of courtiers, some privileged to be seated, others standing, all hanging upon the king's every word. When the king retired for the night, the same formality prevailed as in the morning.

In the early years of his long reign, Louis was tolerant of the Protestants. He tried to persuade them to convert but used no force against them. When persuasion proved unsuccessful, the king grew increasingly angry. Finally he took action. In 1685 he revoked the Edict of Nantes, abolishing the Protestants' religious freedom and political rights. One undesirable result was that thousands of these well-educated, prosperous, skilled, and talented people left France. They were welcomed in many countries of Europe and in North America.

When Louis died in 1715, he left behind an almost bankrupt country. Much of its wealth had been wasted on a series of wars that brought France limited benefits. Louis's incredible extravagance did the rest.

The Coming of the Revolution

Louis XIV outlived both his son and his grandson. He was succeeded by his great-grandson, who reigned as Louis XV. At a time when the

RELIGIOUS BIGOTRY. *Louis XIV, enthroned at right, hears his decree revoking the Edict of Nantes read to his assembled courtiers (Oct. 18, 1685). The decree abolished freedom of worship for non-Catholics.*   Painting by Armand P.M. Dayot (Paris: Flammarion, 1909)

country was changing rapidly and when fundamental changes in the way it was governed were needed, France got a king who was lazy, superstitious, and prejudiced, and who cared little about matters of state.

One day the king was warned that there might be serious trouble if the nation's problems were not resolved. Louis XV only shrugged his shoulders. "*Après moi, le déluge!* ('After me, the flood!'')," he said.

Despite the king's indifference, his reign saw rapid development in trade, industry, and agriculture. Farm production rose steadily, stimulating demand for manufactured goods. By 1790, industrial production had nearly tripled that of 1700. France's trade with the rest of the world, especially her own far-flung colonies, was booming.

New enterprises were bringing wealth to the middle class, or *bourgeoisie.* These bankers, merchants, and manufacturers chafed under the restrictions and inequities of the regime. They felt that it hampered them and taxed them at every turn, without granting them any real political power. All privileges and prestige were tightly held by the aristocrats, the high clergy, and the king.

One example of the king's arbitrary powers was the *lettres de cachet* ("sealed letters"). By simply signing one of these, the king could imprison anyone for as long as he wished, without even stating the charges. Anyone who publicly criticized the regime was likely to spend some time in the king's dungeons.

In the countryside, a series of bad harvests resulted in food shortages, steep price rises, and widespread distress. A population explosion made the situation worse, for there were already thousands of peasants who owned no land. City folk were not much better off, with severe unemployment at a time of mounting food prices.

Almost constant wars were draining the country's already overstrained resources. The rulers of France were determined to halt the constantly expanding power of their traditional enemy, England. A new war broke out in 1755. Known as the Seven Years' War, it was fought in North America, in Europe, in India, and on the seas. (In North America, it was called the French and Indian War.)

The war ended disastrously for the French in 1763. England won control of Canada and India and proved her naval supremacy. The financial situation in France was more desperate than ever.

Despite all its troubles, France in the eighteenth century was a land of unparalleled cultural brilliance. This was the era of the Enlightenment, when the *philosophes* ("philosophers") were defiantly publishing their critiques of the monarchy and aristocracy, along with works praising democracy, freedom, and equality.

Talented artists such as Jean Watteau, François Boucher, and Jean Fragonard were producing magnificent portrayals of upper-class life. Count Georges Buffon, Antoine Lavoisier, and Jean Baptiste Lamarck were among the researchers advancing the frontiers of science.

Louis XV died in 1774. His successor, Louis XVI, was not much of an improvement. A dull and sluggish personality, he could sometimes be deceitful.

Louis XVI married Marie Antoinette, a charming and beautiful Austrian princess. The marriage was far from happy; it was said that he adored her, while she despised him. Fun-loving and reckless, she squandered millions on jewels, gambling, and gifts to her friends and lovers. She was never popular with the French people.

When the American Revolution broke out in 1775, the king's advisers deemed it a splendid opportunity to weaken the British. Though they had little sympathy with the Americans' democratic ideals, they formed an alliance with them. French aid in money, arms, troops, and naval power helped ensure the American victory.

But the French could ill afford such a costly investment. The war doubled the national debt. The only solution was to impose new taxes. Few sources were available. The aristocrats and upper bourgeoisie were exempt from most forms of taxation.

The common people were already taxed to the hilt. They particularly resented such impositions as the *gabelle*, a tax on salt (then indispensable for preserving meats), and the *corvée*, which required them to work for nothing on the king's roads.

No tax reforms were possible without the consent of the upper classes. In 1786 the king therefore summoned the most important nobles, high clergymen, and judges to an Assembly of Notables. His ministers pleaded with them to help ease the government's crushing debt. They arrogantly refused.

The first signs of revolt had already broken out in the countryside. Angry, starving peasants had attacked a few castles and burned tax and land records.

Desperate, the king called for a meeting of the Estates General. This ancient institution supposedly represented all three of France's estates—the churchmen, the nobles, and the common people. It had not met for centuries.

The Estates General met on May 5, 1789. The delegates of the Third Estate were mostly members of the bourgeoisie, with a sprinkling of peasants. They demanded equal representation with the First and Second estates, the nobles and clergy. This was granted almost at once.

Even more important to the Third Estate was its demand for individual voting rather than bloc voting. In bloc voting, each estate would have one vote. The Third Estate would always be outvoted by the other two. Individual voting would mean that the Third Estate could win its demands, for the more liberal members of the aristocracy, as well as the clergymen who lived and worked among the common people, could usually be counted on to vote with them. This demand was refused.

The members of the Third Estate knew they must act. On June 17, to tumultuous cheers and applause, they voted to withdraw from the Estates General. They then declared themselves the National Assembly and invited the upper classes to join.

The French Revolution had begun.

The Era of Revolution

Fall of the Bastille

If Louis XVI had been a wise ruler, he would have understood that the people were in a desperate mood. By June 1789 incidents of violence had already occurred in the countryside. The Third Estate had bolted from the Estates General and declared itself the National Assembly.

But the king was blind to the danger. The National Assembly had barely begun its sessions when he scornfully ordered it locked out of the meeting hall. The members marched over to a nearby indoor tennis court. They swore a solemn oath that they would continue meeting until they had given France a constitution.

The king seemed to give in. He ordered the First and Second Estates

TENNIS COURT OATH. *Having withdrawn from the Estates General, the representatives of the Third Estate swear never to abandon the struggle until France has a constitution. The scene was an indoor tennis court.* Courtesy of French Embassy, Press and Information Division

to join the Third Estate. He even recognized the combined body as a National Constituent Assembly, empowered to write the nation's first constitution.

Louis XVI had not really accepted the need for change. He brought foreign regiments into Paris to crush the challenge to his power. And on July 11 he dismissed the finance minister, Jacques Necker, who had proposed reforms that were supported by the people.

By July 12 angry crowds had formed in many quarters of Paris. Their first target was an armory in the center of the city. There they seized thousands of muskets and twenty cannon. On July 14 newly armed and grimly determined Parisians marched on the Bastille.

This towering fortress was used as a prison, holding both political prisoners and criminals. Over the years, hundreds had been caged in its dungeons on the sole authority of a *lettre de cachet* signed by the king. The people hated the Bastille as a symbol of oppression.

In July 1789 the fortress held only seven prisoners. It was defended by a small force of aging army veterans and Swiss guards. Their commander at first ordered them to resist, but he soon realized it was hopeless. The huge gates were thrown open. The people surged in, freed the prisoners, and started to demolish the Bastille.

Its fall signaled the end of the old regime. Ever since, July 14 has been celebrated each year as Bastille Day, the joyous national holiday of the French Republic.

When Louis XVI was told about the fall of the Bastille, he asked, "But then, is it a revolt?" "No, Sire," he was told. "It is a revolution!"

The Constitutional Monarchy

August 4 was another historic day. The Assembly formally abolished the centuries-old feudal rights and privileges of the aristocracy. All Frenchmen were declared equal before the law.

On August 27 the Assembly adopted the Declaration of the Rights of Man and of the Citizen. Besides guaranteeing freedom of speech, press, and assembly, it established the complete equality of all citizens before the law. Slavery was abolished in all lands under French rule. The Declaration has been incorporated into several of the constitutions that have governed France since then, including the present one.

The work of the Assembly came to a climax with the adoption of a constitution. It retained the monarchy but greatly reduced the king's authority. Lawmaking powers were vested in a new Legislative Assembly. The constitution also set up the system of *départements* that still serves as the basis of local government.

Further radical steps affected the Church. Under a new Civil Constitution of the Clergy, all bishops and priests had to be elected. They were required to swear a "civic oath" of loyalty to the new government. Most drastic of all was the confiscation of Church lands. They were to be sold in order to raise badly needed funds for the revolutionary government.

The Pope condemned these actions and forbade the clergy to swear the required oath. About half did so, however.

On July 14, 1790, in a formal ceremony marking the first anniversary of Bastille Day, King Louis XVI pledged to abide by the constitution. Less than a year later, he led the royal family in an attempt to flee the country. The king was recognized on the way and arrested. The royal family returned to Paris, under guard.

In the National Assembly, conflict raged between the bourgeoisie and the poorer, more radical elements among the revolutionary forces. The latter group seized power. The radicals called for the election of a National Convention to write a new and even more democratic constitution.

The Revolution Goes to War

Meanwhile, revolutionary France faced the united enmity of Europe's monarchies. The Austrian Empire formed an alliance with Prussia specifically aimed at France. In April 1792, fearing invasion, France declared war on these two hostile powers.

The war began with some battlefield reverses for the French. But on September 20 the revolutionary army decisively defeated the Prussians at Valmy, north of Paris. This was one of the rare historic occasions when an army composed largely of volunteers and draftees from the common people had defeated an army of rigorously trained and experienced professionals.

The very next day, emboldened by this military victory, the National Convention abolished the monarchy. September 22 was proclaimed as Day One of Year One of the Republic. The newly rearranged months of the year received descriptive new names. *Fructidor,* for example, signified the harvest month (parts of August and September). *Thermidor* designated the hottest month (July–August), *Nivôse* the snowiest (December–January), *Pluviôse* the rainiest (January–February), and so on.

Three months later, the Convention put King Louis XVI on trial for treason. A large majority found him guilty. He was executed by guillotine (a new device for beheading condemned persons) on January 21, 1793. Queen Marie Antoinette followed him to the guillotine in Octo-

"DEATH TO THE KING!" *Convicted of treason, King Louis XVI was guillotined at the height of the Reign of Terror in 1793. Here the executioner displays the king's head to the people.* Courtesy of French Government Tourist Office. Engraving by Berthoult. Private Collection, Roger Roche, Paris

ber. She had conspired with the rulers of her native Austria and other foreign powers against France.

By that time France was at war against England, the Netherlands, Spain, and Austria. To fight the war on so many fronts, the Convention ordered a *levée en masse* ("mass conscription"). Within a year the *levée* had recruited over a million men, organized into twelve armies. The revolutionary armies were victorious on all fronts. But the coalition of foreign powers persisted in their determination to destroy the Revolution, and the war went on.

The Reign of Terror

Foreign enemies were not the only source of danger. In some of France's western provinces, royalist forces rose up in rebellion and had to be smashed.

Within the Convention, the struggle for power was now between radicals called Jacobins and moderates called Girondins. By midsummer 1793 the Jacobins, led by Maximilien Robespierre and Georges Danton, had won out. They concentrated all power in a Committee of Public Safety. To protect the Revolution against its enemies on all sides, the Committee launched a ruthless campaign of arrests and executions that has come to be called the Reign of Terror. Over a two-year period, about 5,000 aristocrats and others accused of undermining the government were sent to the guillotine.

But soon the Jacobins were at each other's throats. Amid charges and countercharges of betraying the Revolution, Danton, Robespierre, and other Jacobin leaders were tried and executed.

Despite the vicious infighting, the Convention had achieved some remarkable results. It redistributed a considerable amount of land, guaranteed the right of private property, established uniform weights and measures under the metric system, ensured the separation of Church and State, and laid plans for France's first public education system.

Enter Napoleon

Conservatives now took power. Determined to prevent any new revolutionary uprisings organized and led by the Jacobins, they carried out their own Reign of Terror against the radical forces. They then wrote a new constitution, setting up a new government. It consisted of an executive committee of five called the Directory, and a two-house parliament.

A royalist uprising in Paris threatened to overthrow the new government. The Directory called in a young general named Napoleon Bonaparte. He set up a battery of artillery in front of the government building and gave the mob what he later called "a whiff of grapeshot" (a devastating form of cannon fire). The revolt ended almost as soon as it had begun.

Napoleon was rewarded by being given command of the French army in Italy. A victorious campaign there built up his reputation.

In 1798 the Directory sent Napoleon to conquer Egypt, as a way of cutting the British off from their empire in India. Near the town of Rosetta, one of his officers discovered a stone slab inscribed with three kinds of writing. It eventually became known as the Rosetta Stone. At the top were Egyptian hieroglyphics, a form of picture-writing that no one had been able to decipher ever since the disappearance of the ancient Egyptian empire. In the middle was demotic, a simplified form of Egyptian writing. And at the bottom was Greek.

Scholars soon realized that the text was the same in all three languages. But it was not until 1821 that a French archeologist, Jean

François Champollion, succeeded in decoding the hieroglyphics by using the other texts as a key. One of the world's oldest linguistic mysteries had been solved.

Napoleon won a series of land victories in Egypt, but a British fleet destroyed the French fleet in the Battle of the Nile. Napoleon abandoned his army and returned to France.

He joined two members of the Directory in a plot to take power. On November 9, 1799, they staged a successful *coup d'état* ("overthrow of the government").

The plotters devised a new form of government called the Consulate. Napoleon was declared First Consul, to serve for ten years. Two other Consuls would rule with him. The system was modeled on the ancient Roman government of Julius Caesar's time.

The new system was submitted to a vote of the people. They approved it overwhelmingly. Napoleon was now the virtual dictator of France.

Within three years he had himself declared Consul for life. And in 1804 he assumed the supreme title, Emperor Napoleon I.

The First Empire

The Emperor set up a highly centralized government, with all power concentrated in his hands. Each *département* was to be ruled by a prefect personally appointed by him.

Over the next decade Napoleon made many changes. He set up the first system of *lycées* ("senior high schools") supported by the state. He brought order to the chaotic legal system, organizing the nation's laws under the *Code Napoléon*. It incorporated many reforms achieved by the Revolution, such as equality before the law and freedom of religion.

At the same time the Napoleonic Code restricted the rights of women and reinstituted slavery in the colonies. Always uppermost in his mind were the needs of his army, and he spared no expense to ensure its

SELF-CORONATION. *In this painting by Louis David, Napoleon is about to crown his wife, Josephine, as empress. He had already placed the emperor's crown upon his own head.* Courtesy of French Embassy, Press and Information Division

battle-readiness. Napoleon saw himself as a great reformer and bearer of the glorious traditions of the Revolution, but his one-man rule ultimately produced a militaristic tyranny marked by severe limits on human rights.

Napoleon rewarded all who performed outstanding service by naming them to membership in his new *Légion d'honneur* ("Legion of Honor"). It has continued as one of France's proudest awards to the present day.

Napoleon was almost constantly at war as he sought to make France the predominant power in Europe. He proved to be one of the most brilliant military strategists ever. Time and again he defeated forces much larger than his own.

Most experts agree that Napoleon's masterpiece was the Ulm–Austerlitz campaign in the fall of 1805. He faced an Allied force of Austrian and Russian troops numbering about 160,000 men. His own *Grande Armée* had about 75,000 at the start but probably included no more than 60,000 during the climactic battle.

Always an advocate of offensive rather than defensive strategies, he marched his army some 800 miles in thirty days—an unheard-of speed for troops on the march—to surprise his enemies deep in their own territory. A first victory came when he trapped an Austrian army of 70,000, under General Mack, at Ulm. Napoleon outmaneuvered Mack so completely that the Austrian finally had no choice but to surrender.

Continuing his advance, Napoleon carefully scouted the area for a battlefield that would best suit his purposes. He found an ideal area west

VIVE L'EMPEREUR! ("LONG LIVE THE EMPEROR!") *At the peak of his power, Napoleon reviews his troops before the battle of Jena in 1806. Some of the soldiers break ranks to cheer their seemingly invincible commander.* New York Public Library Picture Collection

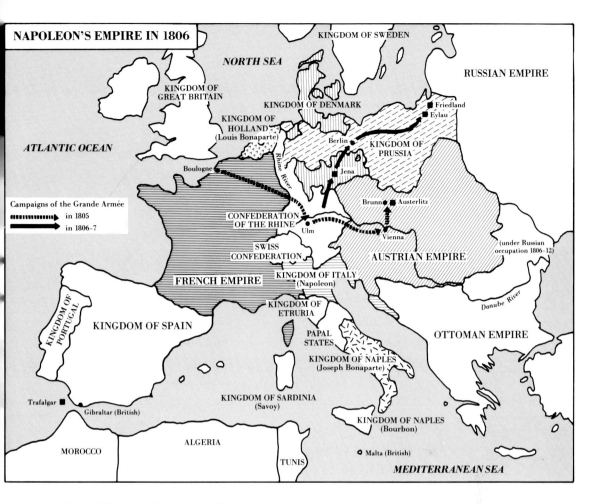

KINGDOM OF SWEDEN

NORTH SEA

RUSSIAN EMPIRE

KINGDOM OF
GREAT BRITAIN

KINGDOM OF DENMARK

Friedland
Eylau

KINGDOM OF
HOLLAND
(Louis Bonaparte)

ATLANTIC OCEAN

Berlin

KINGDOM OF
PRUSSIA

Boulogne

Rhine River

Jena

Campaigns of the Grande Armée
▬▬▬▬▶ in 1805
▬▬▬▶ in 1806–7

CONFEDERATION
OF THE RHINE

Brunn ● Austerlitz

Ulm

SWISS
CONFEDERATION

Vienna

(under Russian
occupation 1806–12)

AUSTRIAN EMPIRE

FRENCH EMPIRE

KINGDOM OF ITALY
(Napoleon)

KINGDOM OF
ETRURIA

Danube River

KINGDOM OF
PORTUGAL

KINGDOM OF SPAIN

PAPAL
STATES

OTTOMAN EMPIRE

KINGDOM OF NAPLES
(Joseph Bonaparte)

Trafalgar ■

KINGDOM OF SARDINIA
(Savoy)

Gibraltar (British)

KINGDOM OF NAPLES
(Bourbon)

MOROCCO

ALGERIA

Malta (British) ○

TUNIS

MEDITERRANEAN SEA

of a village called Austerlitz. It featured an elevated area called the
Pratzen Heights. Napoleon lured the Allies onto this height and then,
faking a retreat, lured them down to attack his apparently defeated
force. The overconfident Allies moved to the attack in not very good
order. Then Napoleon sprang his trap. Suddenly, out of the morning
mists, cheering French forces came storming into the ranks of the
surprised and demoralized Allied troops. The Allied attack quickly
crumbled into a disorderly rout.

The Allies had lost about 27,000 killed, wounded, and missing. The
French had lost fewer than 9,000. Austria was knocked out of the war.
Russia had to ask for an armistice. It was Napoleon's first battle after

becoming Emperor. It made him more popular than ever.

By 1812 France's only rival on the European continent was Russia. Napoleon invaded that country at the head of a formidable army of about 600,000 men. He captured Moscow, but the Russians still refused to surrender. Winter was coming on, and Napoleon ordered a return to France. He sped back to Paris, leaving his army to straggle back through the deadly Russian winter. Hundreds of thousands of men froze, starved, or succumbed to the Russians' constant raids.

The Emperor was never again to know the glory of uninterrupted victories. In 1813 the Allies smashed his army, and he had to give up the throne soon afterward. Napoleon went into exile on the small island of Elba, off the Italian coast.

But he was not through yet. In March 1815 Napoleon escaped from Elba, returned to France, and once again ruled as Emperor. The Allies immediately prepared for war. The climax came in the great three-day battle at Waterloo, in Belgium. No longer the masterly commander of old, Napoleon suffered his final defeat.

This time he was deported all the way to St. Helena, a tiny island off the west coast of Africa. Napoleon died there in 1821.

The Revolutionary era was over. But its spirit lived on in the hearts and memories of the people.

CHAPTER VI

The Shaping of Modern France

The Kings Return

The Bourbon dynasty returned to power, promising to rule as constitutional monarchs. But King Louis XVIII, and then Charles X, tried to restore France to the way it was before the Revolution. The people rose up again in 1830, and the Bourbons had to flee. Louis's reign was known as the July Monarchy, after the month in which he came to power with the assistance of the marquis de Lafayette.

A new king, Louis Philippe, replaced them. He represented the Orléans family, a branch of the Bourbons.

Another insurrection broke out in 1832. It failed, but it became the scene of the climactic episodes of Victor Hugo's world-renowned novel *Les Misérables*. Hugo was profoundly sensitive to social injustice of

LIBERTY LEADING THE PEOPLE. *This famous painting by Romantic artist Eugène Delacroix was inspired by the Revolution of 1830.*   Courtesy of French Embassy, Press and Information Division

every kind. In a brief preface, he declared that he had been moved to write the book by

the three problems of the age—the degradation of man by poverty, the ruin of women by starvation, and the dwarfing of children by physical ruin and spiritual night. . . . So long as ignorance and misery remain on earth, books like this cannot be useless.

The hero of his novel is Jean Valjean, who has spent nineteen years chained to the oar of a galley for the crime of stealing a loaf of bread. After his release he encounters a kindly priest who cures him of his pent-up bitterness. Valjean then tries to live a life devoted to helping others, but he is relentlessly hounded by a vindictive police officer named Javert. Amid the turmoil of the uprising of 1832, Valjean saves Javert's life. The policeman, torn between gratitude to Valjean and his rigid notion of duty, takes his own life.

Hugo, perhaps the supreme example of the French Romantic movement in literature, used this story as the centerpiece for an epic tale thronged with hundreds of characters and vividly depicting the social problems of the time.

Under the liberal rule of Louis Philippe, France experienced a period of commercial and industrial growth and prosperity. But the gap between rich and poor kept widening. Revolution broke out again in 1848. Louis Philippe abdicated.

The Second Republic
and the Second Empire

Bloody street fighting raged over whether the country should be governed by a monarchy or a republic. Finally, the Assembly created a new republic. In the presidential elections, Prince Louis Napoleon Bonaparte won a massive victory. He was the nephew of Napoleon I.

Four years later Louis Napoleon overthrew the republic and had himself proclaimed Emperor Napoleon III. Like his uncle, he wielded all power. Critics and opponents of his rule were jailed, exiled, or silenced by fear. The parliament's powers were reduced.

Napoleon III hoped to expand French power and prestige in the world. He involved France in a series of costly wars. These did achieve limited territorial gains.

He blundered badly, however, when he got embroiled in war with Prussia in 1870. The powerful, fast-moving Prussian armies defeated the French in a devastating six-week campaign. They even captured Napoleon III. He had no alternative but to abdicate and go into exile.

NAPOLEON III. *Like his more famous uncle, Napoleon I, he was at first a hero of those who favored a republic. But once in power, he too made himself emperor.* Courtesy of French Embassy, Press and Information Division

The Prussians imposed a harsh peace treaty. France had to pay an indemnity of 5 billion francs. A Prussian army would occupy the country until it was paid. Worst of all, two French provinces, Alsace and Lorraine, were annexed to the new German Empire.

The end of the Franco-Prussian War was marked by one of the goriest revolutionary episodes in the nation's entire history. Large sections of the Paris populace were increasingly embittered as the rich got richer and the common folk got poorer. They blamed the shameful defeat of France's armies on the hated ruling classes.

A new national government had been elected, but most Parisians rejected it. It was headed by an old-time conservative politician named Adolphe Thiers. Confronted by the rising fury of the city's people, Thiers removed the government from Paris to Versailles.

Inside the capital, a coalition of radicals assumed control. Their views ranged from the extremes of anarchism through various shades of socialism and communism to milder forms of liberalism. They proclaimed a new city government, which they called the Commune of Paris.

During their short time in power (seventy-two days), the Communard leaders passed a wide-ranging but confusing series of enactments. Though some were designed to help the needier classes, their actions showed that these widely feared "Reds" actually had no clear or consistent program.

Their hope was that the rest of the nation would follow their lead in overthrowing the established order. For the defense of the Commune they relied on the National Guard, a semitrained militia raised mostly from the working-class sections of the city.

Meanwhile, Thiers was surrounding the city with the troops of the regular army. During the ensuing siege, the people suffered anew from famine and disease.

In mid-May the government troops broke through the city's defenses. The desperate defenders were driven back from one barricade to another. In an incident that left-wing groups still commemorate each year, 147 Communards captured just before the final surrender were lined up against a wall in the Père Lachaise cemetery and executed. But that was just the beginning. An estimated 20,000 to 25,000 Parisians, mostly workers, suffered the same fate during the next seven days, known as *la semaine sanglante* ("the bloody week"). Thousands of others were shipped off to exile.

The Third Republic

France recovered quickly, both from the blows inflicted by the Prussians and from its brief civil war. The indemnity was paid off within a few years, freeing the country of foreign occupation. But the loss of Alsace and Lorraine was never forgotten. Frenchmen dreamed of the day of *revanche* ("revenge").

Meanwhile the economy prospered. Factories rose everywhere as the advances of the Industrial Revolution were applied. French culture had never been more brilliant or more influential throughout the civilized world.

In literature, the two giants comparable in stature to Hugo were Honoré de Balzac and Émile Zola. Balzac's masterpiece was a multi-volume work called *La Comédie Humaine* (*The Human Comedy*) (1842–1848). It differs from Hugo's novels in that it avoids all sentimentality in favor of a starkly realistic view of human nature.

Zola's novels resemble Hugo's in their sympathy for the downtrodden common people, but Zola strove to construct his stories on a scientific analysis of human behavior. He was deeply influenced by the then-new theories of Charles Darwin, but he also believed that the capitalist system was the root cause of the social evils of his time. He espoused socialism.

One of his novels, *Germinal*, is based on a long and bitter coal-

TO THE BARRICADES! *Troops of the regular army assault a Communard barricade blocking the fashionable Rue de Rivoli, as flames spread through the heart of the city.* Studio Henri, Saint-Brice

MASS EXECUTIONS. *Thousands of supporters of the Paris Commune were executed immediately after the French army recaptured the city from its revolutionary defenders.* L'Établissement Cinématographique et Photographique des Armées à Fort d'lrvy

miners' strike that lasted for months in 1884. At that time the French trade-union movement was weak, and the government had not yet passed any laws to protect the workers.

The miners' leader, Étienne, tries to persuade the mineowner to rescind a wage cut. The owner refuses. Étienne's reply is a pithy expression of Zola's point of view:

We understand very well that our lot will never be bettered as long as things go on as they are going; and that is the reason why some day or another the workers will end by arranging that things shall go differently.

The strike ends in disaster. Étienne moves on, determined to continue the struggle wherever he may be needed.

The nineteenth century was also a golden age for French poetry. A unique figure among the poets was Charles Baudelaire. Profoundly impressed by the haunting melancholy in the poems of Edgar Allan Poe, he translated Poe's works into French. But in his own poetry the hypersensitive Baudelaire went beyond Poe in expressing a morbid sense of inescapable doom. Baudelaire has been described as a forerunner of the twentieth-century surrealists. His spirit breathes through this excerpt from "The Flawed Bell" (translated by Robert Lowell):

> My soul is flawed, and often when I try
> to shrug away my early decrepitude,
> and populate the night with my shrill cry,
>
> I hear the death-cough of mortality
> choked under corpses by a lake of blood—
> my rocklike, unhinging effort to die.

Painting, sculpture, music, and the dance also evidenced the cultural flowering of the nineteenth century. These will be discussed in a later chapter.

If France's literary men spoke with many voices, perhaps it was because the country itself was living through a period filled with contradictions. In 1875 the monarchists and other reactionaries suffered defeat, as the parliament adopted a new democratic constitution that seemed to make France a republic once and for all.

Barely twenty years later the country was once again in the throes of a social upheaval that threatened to turn the clock back. This time the cause was the court-martial, conviction, and exile to Devil's Island of Captain Alfred Dreyfus (described earlier, on pp. 19–20).

Though anti-Semitism was certainly a central issue in the Dreyfus affair, it was not the only issue. On one side, enthusiastically endorsing Dreyfus's conviction, were royalists, aristocrats, ultraconservatives, landowners, and all those who resented the transformation of France into a modern, industrialized, democratic country. Opposing them were those who welcomed progress in all its forms. Thus the Dreyfus case dramatized the conflicts that had divided the French nation since the Revolution—and that remain disruptive in French life today.

By 1900 France ruled the world's second-largest colonial empire, surpassed only by the British. France governed possessions in Africa, South America, southeast Asia, the Caribbean, and the Pacific. But the rising power of Germany threatened French security. Germany boasted a larger population, more highly developed industry, a formidable army, and a growing navy. France sought safety in alliances with Russia and Britain, forming the Triple Entente. The Germans countered with the Triple Alliance, placing Italy and Austria-Hungary on their side.

A clash between these two heavily armed alliance systems was inevitable. World War I broke out in August 1914.

Within a few months the war settled into a bloody slugging match between armies fighting from heavily fortified trenches. Mass attacks by both sides produced only mountains of dead, with advances measured in yards. Northeastern France, where most of the fighting took place, was devastated.

In 1917, just as the French and British armies were nearing exhaustion, the United States entered the war. Soon millions of American "doughboys" were battling alongside the Allies.

Germany surrendered on November 11, 1918. The French were delirious with joy as they hailed the return of Alsace and Lorraine. But the loss of about 1½ million young men left a tragic gap that weakened

INTO NO-MAN'S-LAND. *A combat photographer snapped these French soldiers crossing a trench and advancing through barbed wire, on this typical World War I battlefield.* New York Public Library Picture Collection

the nation and lowered the birth rate for decades. The nation's debts exceeded 150 billion gold francs.

The twenty-year period between the two world wars was a time of governmental instability. and weakness. In the 1930s, faced with the rising menace of Nazi Germany, France was too divided to take decisive action.

On September 1, 1939, Germany invaded Poland. France and Britain declared war. They could do little to help Poland, which was swiftly conquered. In the spring of 1940 Hitler unleashed his new *Blitzkrieg* ("lightning war") tactics upon western Europe. Norway, Denmark, Holland, Belgium, Luxembourg, and France all fell before the seemingly invincible Germans. Britain stood alone.

The Germans divided France into two zones. The north and west, facing England, were occupied by Nazi troops. The southern third was administered by a supposedly independent new French government, with its capital at Vichy in south central France. It was headed by a popular, aged hero of World War I, Marshal Philippe Pétain. The new government collaborated closely with the Germans.

Many of the nation's military and political leaders fled to England and pledged to continue the fight. The leader of these Free French forces was General Charles de Gaulle. Inside France, the Resistance fought the Germans.

In June 1944, when the Allies invaded France, Free French troops formed an important part of the invading armies. As soon as Paris was liberated, de Gaulle headed a provisional government that prepared a new constitution and organized free elections.

In April 1945, France joined the other victorious Allies as a founding member of the United Nations. As one of the five permanent members of its Security Council, France has veto power over decisions affecting world peace and security.

D-DAY. *On June 6, 1944, the Allies launched their long-awaited invasion of Hitler's "Fortress Europe." Above, photographed from their landing craft under fire, American troops assault a Normandy beach.* Courtesy of Library of Congress

DAY OF GLORY. *(Right) On August 25, 1944, at the climax of the battle to liberate Paris after four years of Nazi occupation, the French Resistance fighter at left and the regular army officer at right share the joy of victory.* Courtesy of Seeberger Bros.

19/124
10

Ils se sont
retrouvés après cinquante mois de séparation.
Celui de gauche a mené le combat en France, dans
le clandestinité, risquant chaque jour une mort
anonyme. Il ne portait même plus son vrai nom tant
son avait changé. C'est celui de droite qui le lui
a rendu. Celui-là aussi a continué le combat dès
juillet 1940. Il est parti de Fort-Lamy, il a pris
Kouffra, le Fezzan, Tripoli, Tunis et puis Paris.
Le combattant F.F.I. et le combattant de l'armée
Leclerc s'embrassent dans l'ivresse de la victoire.

The Fourth Republic

The newly constituted government of the Fourth Republic took office in 1946. It resembled the Third Republic in many ways. It too proved highly unstable, with frequent changes of prime ministers.

The Republic's leaders faced especially difficult dilemmas in the foreign-policy realm. The most urgent problem affected relations with the colonies. They were demanding independence. Within a few years the French had granted it to several African colonies.

The French hoped to retain control of Indochina (consisting of Vietnam, Laos, and Cambodia). There a Communist-led nationalist movement launched a guerrilla campaign against the French in 1946. The long, bitter war lasted till 1954. France had to abandon the area, only to see the Americans renew the fight in Vietnam about ten years later.

The North Vietnamese military commander, General Giap, whose strategy produced the disastrous French defeat in the climactic 1954 battle of Dien Bien Phu, also masterminded the campaigns that resulted in the American departure from Vietnam twenty years later.

Rebellion also erupted in the one North African colony still under French rule, Algeria. Once again, French troops were engaged in a costly and futile war.

France took an active part in the formation of closer ties among the nations of the free world. It was one of the twelve founding members of NATO (the North Atlantic Treaty Organization) in 1949. In 1957 it joined five other west European countries to form the Common Market, whose membership has doubled since then.

After the catastrophes of two world wars, France's leaders were convinced that peace could be assured only if the nations of Europe yielded some portion of their national sovereignty. Accordingly, France became a major force behind the formation of the European Parliament.

Its ten member countries have granted it only limited powers as yet, but it has excellent prospects of developing into a power in international politics. Since 1979, the delegates have been elected by universal suffrage in all ten countries.

Simone Weil, one of France's most distinguished jurists and cabinet ministers, was the first woman elected president of the European Parliament. She served from 1979 to 1982.

The Fifth Republic

For years, de Gaulle had demanded a new constitution. He believed that the country's chronic political instability could be ended by a new government headed by a powerful president. By 1958 the country's need for a strong leader was urgent. France was badly divided over the war in Algeria. There was a strong possibility of a *coup d'état* by army commanders.

De Gaulle got his wish. The constitution of the Fifth Republic concentrated a considerable measure of power in the president's hands. The general was elected.

Ignoring the demands of the more extreme army men, de Gaulle brought the war to an end and granted Algeria its independence in 1962. France was at peace for the first time in twenty-three years.

There followed a period of economic boom and modernization. The new prosperity was not shared equally by all segments of the population, however. University students were particularly discontented. They felt that the education system was rigid and outmoded and that their job prospects were poor.

In May 1968 students at the Paris universities went on strike. Their fellow students all over the country quickly joined them. They demanded not only educational reforms but changes in society aimed at greater social equality and improved employment opportunities. Violence erupted on many campuses, with pitched battles between students and police.

These outbreaks were almost certainly influenced by the example of the student movement in the United States. Beginning in the early 1960s, American students had played an increasingly militant role in the agitation for civil rights and against the Vietnam war. But the student uprisings of 1968 were very much in line with a Paris tradition dating back at least 200 years. The revolutionary movements that had broken out periodically ever since the great Revolution of 1789 had almost invariably involved active, large-scale participation by the city's always restless and unruly students. Their lead was usually followed by students in France's other university centers.

Gradually at first, but then in ever-mounting numbers, the workers joined the movement. Eventually some 10 million workers took part in this nationwide social upheaval.

Both students and workers won some improvements. A start was made on the educational reforms that have produced the modernized system of the present. Workers' wages, working conditions, and the legal status of unions were all bettered.

De Gaulle called an election to test the impact of the movement on his Government. He and his party won reelection by a large majority. Barely a year later, he proposed a new wave of reforms. When the Assembly rejected these, he resigned.

The decade of the 1970s was a time of mounting economic distress. A worldwide oil crisis started in 1973, with severe effects on the French economy. By 1981 there were about 1½ million unemployed, and the

STUDENTS IN REVOLT. *In May 1968 students at universities throughout France demonstrated for radical change in the educational and political system. Some, like the woman in the picture, brandished the black flag of anarchy.* Courtesy of *Paris Match*

number was rising. Economic growth had fallen from an average annual rate of 5 to 6 percent to a bare 1 to 2 percent.

These difficulties produced a marked change in public opinion. In the 1981 election, the voters elected a Socialist majority to Parliament for the first time. At first the Socialists followed their traditional policy of nationalizing major enterprises and redistributing the wealth. But the economy stayed sluggish. The Socialists then adopted austerity policies similar to those favored by the conservatives.

In the parliamentary election of 1986, the conservatives won a majority. Socialist President François Mitterrand had to share power temporarily with a conservative prime minister. But Mitterrand won a resounding victory in the presidential election of 1988. He was then able to govern once more with a Socialist prime minister and Council of Ministers.

The politicians were in a quandary. Public opinion kept shifting in perplexing ways. Whichever party won power in future elections, the only safe prediction was that the individualistic French would remain unpredictable.

The Land:
Fertility and Variety

France is the largest country in western Europe. Its area equals that of Great Britain, West Germany, Belgium, and Holland combined. Comparison with the United States shows that it is not quite as big as Texas.

The country extends over an area of 212,918 square miles (551,602 square kilometers). It stretches 594 miles (950 kilometers) from north to south and about the same distance from east to west.

France is situated along the westernmost edge of the European continent. With 1,920 miles (3,200 kilometers) of coastline, half of its borders are oceanic. Its shape is roughly that of a hexagon.

To the west lies the Atlantic Ocean, with its Bay of Biscay on the southwest. The English Channel (called *La Manche* by the French)

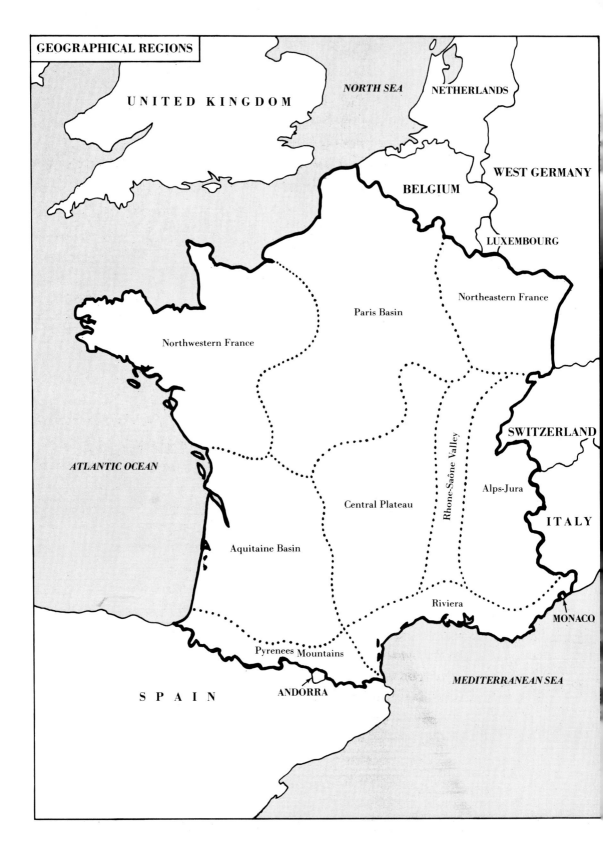

GEOGRAPHICAL REGIONS

UNITED KINGDOM

NORTH SEA

NETHERLANDS

WEST GERMANY

BELGIUM

LUXEMBOURG

Northeastern France

Paris Basin

Northwestern France

ATLANTIC OCEAN

SWITZERLAND

Rhône-Saône Valley

Alps-Jura

ITALY

Central Plateau

Aquitaine Basin

Riviera

MONACO

Pyrenees Mountains

ANDORRA

MEDITERRANEAN SEA

S P A I N

forms the northwest border. At its narrowest point the Channel divides France from England by a mere 22 miles (35 kilometers).

Bounding France on the north and northeast are Belgium, Luxembourg, and West Germany. These are the only French boundaries that are unprotected by any natural barrier, except for a relatively short stretch where the Rhine River flows between France and West Germany. Invaders have traditionally chosen these open borders as the easiest routes of entry into France.

Switzerland and Italy lie to the east and southeast, separated from France by the Jura and Alps mountains. On the south, the spectacular coastline faces the Mediterranean Sea. Finally, on the southwest, the Pyrenees mountains form a rugged natural boundary between France and Spain.

The terrain of France is extremely varied. It includes snow-covered mountain ranges and spacious, fruitful plains that cover two thirds of the territory. Forests clothe about a quarter of the country. Four great river systems water and drain the richly diverse and fertile soils. A fifth river, the Rhine, flows along only the eastern border.

Nine Geographical Regions

The French landscape is so varied that an accurate description requires breaking it down into nine separate categories.

1. The Paris Basin
The Paris Basin occupies north central France. This vast fertile plain is one of the world's richest farming areas. Grounded on a shallow limestone basin, it is ringed with extensive oak and beech forests that are termed "the lungs of Paris."

The city of Paris has played a unique role in French life. Ever since the Middle Ages, it has been not only the nation's capital, but also the leading center of culture, learning, the arts, fashion, commerce, and industry. It is, of course, world-famous for its many beautiful monuments, superb museums, and broad boulevards lined with stately buildings.

The city was not always so attractive. It was for many centuries a place of narrow, crowded, unsanitary streets in which travel was difficult and unpleasant. It was not until the time of Emperor Napoleon III, in the 1850s and 1860s, that a massive program of demolition and rebuilding was decreed. The job was given to Baron Georges Haussmann, who cleared away vast slum areas in order to widen many streets and create the network of boulevards.

Cleaning up the city and beautifying it were only a part of the Emperor's purpose. He also wanted to be able to move his troops quickly to deal with Paris's rebellious mobs.

In times of political upheaval, Parisians have always been the ones to spark movements fighting to overthrow the established order. Regarding themselves as more knowledgeable and sophisticated than the people out in the provinces, they have come to assume that the rest of the country will follow their lead. The provincials have often tended to resent what they regard as Parisian arrogance and radicalism.

The region surrounding Paris is called the Ile-de-France (Island of France). The name reflects the fact that it is bounded by three rivers, the Seine, the Oise, and the Marne.

Beginning in the mid-nineteenth century, the gentle landscapes of the Ile-de-France have attracted many of France's most renowned artists. Seeking to escape the limitations of studio art in favor of painting from nature, the Impressionists were the first to move out of Paris as a group. Among those who lived and worked in the Ile-de-France for varying periods were such well-known painters as Pierre Auguste Renoir, Claude Monet, and Camille Pisarro. They were later followed by the

Postimpressionists, most notably Paul Cézanne.

The entire road and railway network of France centers on Paris, which is also the country's main hub of international aviation. The navigable Seine River flows westward through the city to the Atlantic, providing still another heavily used means of transportation.

Paris and its suburbs and the Basin's other towns and cities lead the country in industrial production. A second industrial district of the Paris Basin is in the north, along the Belgian border. It contains France's principal coalfields. Today these centuries-old coal mines are increasingly difficult and expensive to work. Oil and nuclear power are replacing them.

The largest city in the north is Lille, for many years a great center of textile manufacturing. Today that industry, too, is in decline.

Along the coast to the west are some of France's most important seaports: Boulogne, Calais, Dieppe, and Dunkirk.

The principal farm crops of the region are wheat, oats, sugar beets, potatoes, turnips, and animal fodder. The largest wheat-growing area is the broad plain of the Beauce, in the southwestern section of the Basin. Wheat is produced in such abundance that large quantities are exported.

The Basin's southern section includes the upper valley of the Loire River. Often dubbed "the garden of France," the valley is world-famous for its magnificent châteaux in settings of captivating scenic beauty. It is also noted for its excellent white wines.

Even better known as one of the world's premier wine-growing areas is the nearby province of Burgundy. It lies east of the Loire valley. Few red wines produced anywhere are more cherished than those that bear Burgundy labels.

Burgundy has a proud history as a province whose ruling dukes were often more wealthy and powerful than the kings of France. Burgundians today still display a sturdy independence of mind. They are an earthy, realistic, physically tough people with round, smiling faces and a tendency to mischief. They love to argue and are known for their eloquence in dispute.

As have several other French provinces, Burgundy has revived a number of old folk customs in recent years. One of these is the *cousinerie*, in which villagers are invited as "cousins" to join in some copious wine drinking in the winegrowers' cellars.

Another traditional festival features water jousting on the Yonne River during the summer. Two young men of the region, armed with sturdy poles and shields, station themselves on platforms aboard long boats. As the boats are rowed toward each other at full tilt, each man tries to knock his opponent into the water, somewhat in the manner of medieval knights jousting on horseback with lances.

Burgundy is almost as famous for its food as for its wines. The province holds a gastronomic fair in November, at which its chefs—both amateur and professional—compete.

Still another district renowned for its vineyards is the province of Champagne, forming the Paris Basin's easternmost section. Its gently rolling terrain and chalky soil are ideal for cultivation of the grapes from which the celebrated sparkling wine that bears the province's name is produced. Its northern tip is covered by the thick forests of the Argonne and the Ardennes. American soldiers fought costly battles here in both world wars.

2. Northeastern France

Northeastern France consists mainly of the provinces of Alsace and Lorraine. The northern edge of the region comprises part of the Ardennes, a thickly wooded area gashed by steep and narrow river gorges.

The province of Lorraine is formed of a rather bleak plateau broken by steep hills and valleys. It contains iron ore deposits that were once among the world's richest. They provided the basis for a third area of heavy industry. Today the iron mines are nearing exhaustion. Huge steel mills and other factories have closed down, and the government is taking measures to alleviate the resulting unemployment.

Running through the area in a roughly north-south direction are the Vosges Mountains. They slope eastward through vineyard-covered hills down to the Rhine River. Besides offering an avenue for trade, the Rhine also provides the area with hydroelectric power. Rhine valley farms produce foodstuffs, dairy products, and wines.

FROM THE BOWELS OF THE EARTH. *These men are preparing to bring up potash from a mine in Alsace.* U. N. Photo

ANCIENT TRADITION. *Peasants in traditional folk costumes of the Vosges hill country listen as the mighty mountain horn is sounded.*   Courtesy of French Cultural Mission

Nancy, capital of Lorraine, and Strasbourg, capital of Alsace, are the region's two principal cities. With their beautiful old buildings and famous universities, they are leading tourist and cultural centers. Strasbourg is the meeting place of the Council of Europe.

The people of Lorraine reflect their generally hard lives in that they tend to be rather reserved and taciturn. Their gray stone houses often stand along rough unpaved roads.

Alsatians, on the other hand, are a talkative, friendly, hospitable people. Their houses and furniture are bright with color. Flowers abound. Many of the houses are in the handsome half-timbered style. They love to gather for storytelling, folksinging, and robust argument in the many *cafés à vin* ("wine cafés") that dot the areas where they grow their famous Rhine wines.

Alsace hosts several festivals each year. The best known is the medieval festival at Ribeauvillé. It features simulated bearbaiting, lords and ladies in elaborate finery on horseback, armor-clad knights jousting, and colorful processions.

3. The Rhone-Saône Valley   Southward lies the Rhone-Saône valley. For the diverse peoples who, over the centuries, have approached France by way of the Mediterranean, this narrow valley has been the traditional entryway.

Once completely uncontrolled and unnavigable, the Rhone has been tamed by a series of multipurpose projects built mostly since World War II. They provide flood control, hydroelectric power, irrigation, and improved navigability. The Donzère-Mondragon project in the lower valley, for example, includes not only dams and power stations but canals and locks as well.

Because the Rhone valley receives relatively little rainfall, the farms have to rely on irrigation systems using water drawn from the river. Vegetable truck gardens are an important source of revenue. Vineyards on the slopes to the west of the river produce fine Burgundy-like wines.

Lyons is the valley's most important city. It dates back to the time of the ancient Gauls. Today it ranks as France's second city.

Lyons became a center of the silk trade in the fifteenth century. Later, when it was discovered that silk could be cultivated in the valley, the city became the world's leading silk-manufacturing center. But French silk culture declined, and in recent times a large part of the fabric for the rich Lyons brocades and other silken fabrics has had to be imported from the Far East. The city has also become a first-rank producer of synthetic fabrics.

The Lyonnais take pride in their city's reputation as a world capital of good eating. At any time of year, gourmets from the entire world throng to the city's many high-rated restaurants. It was a native of Lyons, the renowned chef Anthelme Brillat-Savarin (1755–1826), who said, "Tell me what you eat and I'll tell you who you are."

4. The Alps-Jura Region

The mountainous Alps-Jura region is directly east of the Rhone valley. It borders on Switzerland and Italy.

The Jura area forms the northern section of the region. It rises from the Saône valley through a series of plateaus to a range of moderately high mountains on the border. About 40 percent of the area is forest. Herds of cattle graze in lush upland pastures in summer and in the valleys in winter.

Rising to the south are the lofty French Alps. Their most spectacular feature is the Massif du Blanc, a range of peaks over 13,000 feet (4,000 meters) high. The range culminates in the famous Mont Blanc, highest of all at 15,781 feet (4,782 meters). Nearby is the awe-inspiring *Mer de Glace* ("Sea of Ice"), an immense glacier. Jewel-like lakes dot the region.

Living as they do under conditions of climatic extremes, the people of these regions are known for their realism, toughness, and frugality. They tend to a more devout Catholicism than their countrymen elsewhere and are generally conservative in their politics. Standing apart from the general population are the region's watchmakers, who have long had a reputation for favoring socialism or anarchism.

Abundant hydroelectric power fuels the region's varied industries. But it is best known as one of the world's most popular tourist resort areas. It offers unrivaled scenery, superb skiing and mountain-climbing facilities, and hotels ranging from the most luxurious to more humble no-frills types.

HIGH-ALTITUDE HAMLETS. *Tiny, remote villages dot one of the many picturesque valleys in the Alpine region near the Swiss border.*   Courtesy of French Cultural Mission

5. The Central Plateau

Largest of the geographic regions, sprawling across south central France, is the forbidding, thinly populated Massif Central, or Central Plateau. It takes up one sixth of the entire country.

The Massif is a region of high granite plateaus cut by many gorges. The plateaus range as high as 4,000 to 5,000 feet (1,200 to 1,500 meters). Scattered among them can be found a peculiar feature known as the *puys*, a range of peaks that seem to jut abruptly out of the earth like so many long fingers. Some reach well above the average level of the plateaus. They are all that remain of extinct volcanoes.

Hot mineral springs bubble up at numerous points in this region. Health resorts or spas have been built around them. The largest is at

LE PUY. *This volcanic core or* puy, *about 260 feet (78 meters) high, is typical of many in the Massif Central. The chapel of St.-Michel-d'Aiguihle perches precariously atop it.*
Courtesy of French Embassy, Press and Information Division

Vichy, France's temporary capital during World War II. Its mineral waters are exported to many countries.

Stock raising is carried on throughout the area. A well-known local specialty is Roquefort cheese, made from sheep's milk and popular among gourmets all over the world. Roquefort-sur-Soulzon, the village where the cheese is produced, sits atop a lofty cliff. The cheese is aged in deep caves, noted for their high humidity and cool, even temperatures all year—46° F (8° C). A penicillin fungus that grows naturally in the caves is added to the cheese to produce its unique flavor. The process dates back to Roman times.

At the heart of the Massif is the province of Auvergne. The hardy but poverty-stricken Auvergnats are said to typify the old-time French peasant: somber, hardworking, exceptionally thrifty, suspicious of strangers.

Folk traditions are very much alive here. A favorite is the *bourrée*, a jig, probably Celtic in origin, danced by both men and women with constantly changing partners. Purists do it to the music of the *vielle*, a type of viol, and the *cabrette*, similar to the bagpipe.

The region's chronic unemployment problem has led to massive emigration. Most have moved to Paris, where Auvergnats own or manage an estimated 60 percent of all the cafés. Some parts of the Massif have been virtually depopulated.

6. Northwestern France

Northwestern France is dominated by the rocky Armorican Plateau. The area is largely taken up by the provinces of Normandy and Brittany. Each forms a peninsula protruding into the Atlantic. Most of the land is less than 600 feet (180 meters) above sea level, though there are a few hills—the eroded remains of ancient mountains—that rise as high as 1,400 feet (420 meters).

Normandy is famous for raising fine brindled cattle and superior horses. The herds graze in fields enclosed by live hedgerows of trees and bushes known as *bocages.* The milk of Norman cattle is unusually creamy, with a high fat content that is perfect for fatty cheeses such as Camembert, as well as the rich, slightly salty Normandy butter.

Normandy boasts extensive apple orchards. They produce a special variety of the fruit too small and bitter-tasting for eating. These apples are used for cider and calvados, a potent alcoholic beverage.

Rouen, Normandy's capital, is on the Seine River about 31 miles (50 kilometers) from the Atlantic. The Seine has been dredged from its mouth on the Atlantic all the way to Rouen, so that oceangoing ships

MONT SAINT-MICHEL. *A medieval abbey that has been called "the finest Gothic monument to God's glory built anywhere on earth" crowns this tiny island just off the coast of Normandy.* The Bettmann Archive

can sail right up to the city. Cargoes are then transferred to barges for the journey to Paris.

Two of France's greatest seaports, serving the transatlantic trade, are in Normandy: Le Havre and Cherbourg.

Normandy was separated from the rest of France twice during the Middle Ages. From the ninth century until 1204 it was an independent province heavily colonized by Northmen from Scandinavia. For part of that time, starting in 1066, it was linked to England. The English reconquered it during the Hundred Years' War, only to lose it back to France in 1450.

Partly as a result of this unique history, Normans tend to differ noticeably from their countrymen in physical appearance. Many of them are taller than the average French citizen, with a higher frequency of blond hair and blue eyes.

Their personality, too, is different—calmer, more phlegmatic. Normans have a reputation for extreme prudence, always taking both sides of any question. Asked about the weather, a typical Norman is likely to reply, "Well, it could be better—but it could be worse."

Brittany presents a much bleaker landscape. Large areas are too rocky and barren for cultivation, though they do supply sparse grazing for horses and cattle. Farming can be conducted only on the level coastal plains and in a few fertile inland basins. The main crop is vegetables, but the soil is often thin and the farms poor. Food processing is a growing industry.

SPECTACULAR COAST. *An undaunted fisherman confronts the stormy Atlantic at one of the shoreline's many scenic locations.* Photo by Jean Gaumy; Copyright Magnum Photos

Many of the hardy Bretons make their living from the sea, though the fishing industry is in decline. Along the rocky 2,000-mile coast, tiny fishing villages nestle in sheltered coves. From St. Malo, on the north coast, fishing fleets still brave the Atlantic to reach the cod fisheries off Newfoundland. St. Nazaire contains France's largest shipyards. One of the country's main naval bases is at Brest.

Brittany is France's only Celtic province. Small numbers of Celts settled there in the sixth century B.C. Much larger Celtic forces invaded from Britain almost 1,000 years later. They brought tales of King Arthur and his court with them. The Bretons adapted these to their own locale, placing them in the forests around Rennes. The legends still persist.

BRETON FERRY. *The ticket-taker watches as passengers hurry to board one of the many ferries on the coast of Brittany.* Photo by Guy Le Querrec; Copyright Magnum Photos

Conscious that their region was not annexed into France until the sixteenth century, some Bretons remain stubbornly nationalistic, agitating for independence from France. A tiny extremist group has even been involved in violent action against the government.

Other groups are trying to revive the ancient culture, especially the Celtic language. For many centuries the French government actively suppressed it in the interest of national unity. This policy has now been abandoned. Elective courses in Celtic are available to interested students in Brittany's high schools.

The Bretons share Celtic with the Irish and the Welsh. The language was once spoken throughout the province. As recently as 1930 1.2 million Bretons could speak it, but today less than half that number can. Most Celtic speakers are elderly. The future of the language is at best uncertain.

Brittany is the most ardently Catholic region in all France. Its rate of church attendance is double the national average.

7. The Riviera   The best-known section within the Mediterranean region is the spectacularly scenic Riviera, with its mountains sloping abruptly down to the coastal plain and the popular beaches.

Nice and Cannes are the largest resort cities. Others include Antibes, St. Tropez, and Juan-les-Pins. Not far from the Italian border is glamorous Monte Carlo, capital of the tiny independent principality of Monaco. The hill villages of this area were built on the heights centuries ago for safety and sanitation. The modern population lives mostly in the lowlands.

France's busiest seaport, Marseilles, stands between the Riviera and the Rhone River. It is in constant competition with Lyons for the title of second-largest city in the country. Marseilles is the principal focus of trade between France, the Mediterranean region, and the vast world

SEA HUNT. *On the coast near Marseilles, a sardine fisherman mends his nets.* Photo by Richard Kalvar; Copyright Magnum Photos

to the south and east. The city is heavily industrialized.

Marseilles is well known for its flavorful southern cuisine. An especially popular local specialty is *bouillabaisse*, a savory fish stew.

A short distance to the east lies the naval base of Toulon.

The mild Mediterranean climate ensures farmers a longer growing season than elsewhere. The lower valley of the Rhone is France's richest garden area, producing peaches, melons, strawberries, and asparagus. The area surrounding the town of Grasse is famous for its flowers, basis of the renowned perfume industry. Olive and almond groves that are hundreds of years old abound in the region.

The Rhone carries tons of soil and stones that are constantly added to its delta. The rich loam of the delta forms a natural base for rice culture. A unique breed of white horses is raised in a nearby area called the Camargue.

West of the Rhone is an area devoted mostly to vineyards. They produce grapes suitable only for *vin ordinaire*, a good but inexpensive type of wine that is rarely exported.

Inland lies Provence, a region rich in history and tradition. Its hospitable people are mostly swarthy, stocky, and quick-tempered but equally quick to forgive. They speak French with a marked accent. Older folk in the remoter mountain areas still speak the soft and melodious language called Provençal. It is a version of Occitan, the tongue spoken throughout the region in medieval times. Occitan was the language of the troubadours, the traveling adventurers who roamed from town to town and castle to castle in the Middle Ages, performing their songs and poetry and reciting their stories.

There exists an impressive literature in Provençal, but few writers use the language today. Frédéric Mistral, the most famous of all Provençal poets, led the movement to revive it as a literary language in the nineteenth century. Mistral won the Nobel Prize in Literature in 1904.

Provence boasts numerous towns rich in Roman ruins and medieval buildings. Notable among these are Avignon, Aix, Arles, and Nîmes.

Dotting the hills are many old fortified villages, located on the heights for protection against the Saracen pirates and other marauders of ancient and medieval times. Outsiders find their narrow winding streets, alleys, and archways quaint and picturesque, but many villages are dead or dying. Their people have moved to the towns and cities in the valleys in search of jobs. Some more fortunate villages are experiencing a revival, as outsiders from cities all over France have established second homes here.

The area benefits from a special quality of brilliant daylight, which has attracted many distinguished artists. Towns such as Gordes, St.

FAVORITE SUBJECT. *The Postimpressionist painter Paul Cézanne painted Mont Saint-Victoire, a mountain in Provence, over and over in all seasons and at all times of the day. Each version was different.* The Metropolitan Museum of Art, Bequest of Mrs. H.O. Havemeyer, 1929. The H.O. Havemeyer Collection, (29.100.64)

Paul, and Cagnes-sur-Mer have become artists' colonies. Famous artists who have lived and worked in Provence at various times have included Cézanne, Van Gogh, Picasso, Renoir, Matisse, Dufy, and Chagall.

Provençal cooking is one of the area's chief attractions. Food prepared *à la provençale* is usually cooked in a tomato-and-garlic sauce. Olive oil, not butter, is the starting point.

Bullfighting is a popular sport here. A unique form of it called the *course à la cocarde* can be seen in Arles. Rosettes are stuck on the bull's horns; the difficult and dangerous object is not to kill the bull, as in regular bullfighting, but to snatch the rosettes away.

The men of the region can be observed at almost any time of the day or evening enjoying the highly skilled game of *pétanque.* In this form of bowling, two opposing teams (usually two or three men each) roll metal balls across a dirt-floored court, aiming to place them as close to a target ball as possible without touching it.

Sharing the Mediterranean climate is the French island of Corsica (Corse), about 120 miles (190 kilometers) to the southeast. This mountainous, heavily forested locale permits little farming. Its people fish, raise livestock, and work in the local industries fueled by hydroelectric power. Napoleon I was born here.

Corsicans are a friendly but hot-tempered people. Their fierce loyalties to their families and clans are legendary. Disputes between members of rival families can turn into bitter, long-lasting feuds or vendettas, sometimes culminating in violence and even assassination.

Here too, as in Brittany, a small extremist minority of nationalists is demanding independence from France. They have been responsible for terrorist actions aimed at the authorities.

8. The Aquitaine Basin

The gently rolling Aquitaine Basin occupies the area of southwestern France between the Massif Central and the Atlantic. Most of the Basin is drained by the Garonne River and its tributaries. Fruit orchards and vineyards fill the Garonne valleys.

The river flows in a northwesterly direction to the superb harbor of Bordeaux. This seaport and industrial city has oil refineries, steel mills, and chemical factories. It has given its name to the famous Bordeaux wines produced from the nearby vineyards. Grapes grown in the Cognac district to the north and in the Armagnac district to the south are the raw material for well-known brandies. A futuristic international city of wine and spirits is under construction amid the eighteenth-century buildings of Bordeaux.

WINE TASTING. *In a wine cellar of the Loire valley, an expert prepares to sample one of the choice wines of France.* Courtesy of French Embassy, Press and Information Division

East of Bordeaux is a small agricultural district known as the Périgord. It is famous among gourmets for two specialties: *foie gras*, a delectable appetizer made from goose livers, and truffles, a mushroom-like delicacy.

An area known as the Landes stretches some 150 miles (240 kilometers) south of Bordeaux and 60 miles (96 kilometers) inland. Until the nineteenth century, it was an unhealthy, marshy plain. Sand blowing from its huge coastal dunes blew to the east, menacing the vineyards. The sands have since been anchored through the planting of pine and oak trees, forming France's largest forest. Some dunes can still be seen along the shore; they are the most massive in Europe, some over 330 feet (100 meters) high.

The Aquitaine is still another part of France with its own distinctive past. It was a separate kingdom for much of its early history. Charlemagne named his son Louis king of the province in 780. Later, starting in the twelfth century, it came under English rule. France did not win possession until 1453, at the end of the Hundred Years' War.

Toulouse, in the southeastern Aquitaine, was the original capital of the kingdom, but separated from it in the Middle Ages. The city was ruled by the Counts of Toulouse, the most powerful feudal lords in medieval France.

Today the city is the headquarters of France's burgeoning aerospace industry.

In the southernmost section of the Aquitaine, on the Atlantic coast and in the foothills of the Pyrenees, lives a unique group, the Basques. They are a race apart from any in France or indeed any in Europe. Their place of origin is unknown. They have inhabited the area since at least the early Middle Ages; some scholars believe they have been there even longer. Their language is believed to be the oldest in Europe, but it is unrelated to any other.

There are about a million Basques, but 90 percent of them live across the border in Spain. The Spanish Basques are fervent nationalists, and for many years they have conducted an often violent campaign for independence against the Spanish government. The French Basques too are nationalistic, but they are decidedly less extreme than those of Spain. They are known to help their Spanish brothers by smuggling arms and money to them and by hiding them when they have to flee their country.

9. The Pyrenees Mountains

The Pyrenees mountains loom up south of the Aquitaine Basin. They form a range running nearly 280 miles (450 kilometers) in an east-west direction. With their many peaks

PASTORAL SCENE. *In the summertime, sheep are herded up to the high pastures in the shadow of the snow-clad Pyrenees Mountains.*   Courtesy of French Cultural Mission

rising above 10,000 feet (3,000 meters), the Pyrenees make a formidable barrier between France and Spain.

On the western slopes, which receive abundant rainfall, grasses and trees grow all the way up to the snow line. Cattle and sheep graze along these hillsides. Small farms nestle in the fertile valleys.

Centrally located in the foothills is the town of Lourdes (see photo p. 119), site of a grotto shrine that millions of Roman Catholic pilgrims visit each year. The waters of its spring are believed to have miraculous healing powers.

The Pyrenees' rich hydroelectric potential has been tapped by numerous dams and power stations to provide energy for both local and distant industries.

The Land:
Man and Nature at
Work

Six Climates

France is located in the middle of the north temperate zone. Most of the country enjoys a moderate climate, but it varies across six zones. Extremes are experienced in the mountainous regions and along the eastern borders.

1. The Northwestern Region   The northwestern region, where the provinces of Brittany and Normandy jut out into the Atlantic, has an oceanic climate. Westerly winds blowing in from the sea carry abundant moisture, which ensures rainfall 200 days each year. The Gulf Stream flows northward off the coast, warming the ocean and moderating the climate on shore. Winters are mild, with average January temperatures of 44° F (7° C). The cool summers rarely range above 60° F (16° C).

2. The Aquitaine Basin

In the Aquitaine Basin to the southwest, the oceanic climate is moderated by the southerly location and lower-lying terrain. Temperatures are milder and rainfall slightly lower than in the northwest zone.

3. The Transitional Region

A broad strip of land running through the center of the country from the northern border nearly to the Mediterranean has a transitional climate. Conditions here are balanced between those of the oceanic zone to the west and the continental zone to the east. At the heart of this zone, in the Paris Basin, the average annual temperature is 53° F (12° C). Rainfall totals a moderate 24 inches (60 centimeters) per year, most of it in the summer.

4. The Eastern Region

The climate of eastern France is of the more rigorous continental type. Winds from the east and north bring long, severe winters and stormy summers. Strasbourg, the largest city in Alsace, has near-freezing average temperatures in January and rises to 66° F (19° C) in July. Rainfall varies from 24 to 48 inches (60 to 120 centimeters).

5. The Mountain Areas

Most rigorous of all is the climate in the mountain areas of France—the Pyrenees in the southwest, the Jura and Alps in the east. Many of the peaks are snow-covered all year long. Winters are long, cold, and snowy, while summers are hot and stormy. Some areas, mainly those at higher altitudes, have only two seasons: eight months of winter and four months of summer. Rain and snow are heaviest on the western slopes, which receive the moist winds from the west. The western Pyrenees, for example, have recorded as much as 80 inches (200 centimeters) in some years.

6. The Mediterranean Zone   France's warmest climate affects the southeast or Mediterranean zone. It includes the world-famous resort area known as the Riviera or Côte d'Azur ("Azure Coast"). Summers are dry and hot, with daytime temperatures frequently in the range of 90° F (32° C) or above. In January the thermometer never even approaches the freezing level. This is also the driest region, with rainfall seldom exceeding 20 inches (50 centimeters). What rain there is comes mainly in the fall, often in sudden downpours. A climatic feature peculiar to the Mediterranean region is the *mistral*, a cold, dry wind that blows down the long, narrow valley of the Rhone River almost every day. It has been known to attain hurricane force for three to four days on end.

Rivers and Canals

The five principal rivers of France flow into four seas: the North Sea, the English Channel, the Atlantic, and the Mediterranean. Practically every part of the country is watered by its own river system, a fact that helps to explain the fertility of the land. At various times in French history, the river basins were the centers of independent countries.

The rivers are linked through a remarkable system of canals totaling over 3,000 miles (4,800 kilometers). The *péniches* ("barges") on these canals carry over 75 million tons of industrial and farm products in some years. That amounts to about 6 percent of the total merchandise shipped.

The canals provide an inexpensive way to ship the grain of the north as far south as Marseilles, for example, or the iron ore of Lorraine to the Channel ports. Costs are about half those of railways and a little more than a quarter those of trucks. Specially fitted passenger barges also carry tourists on leisurely tours of the French heartland.

1. The Loire River

Longest of the rivers is the Loire, which runs 634 miles (1,020 kilometers) and drains a large part of central France. Its source is in the Massif Central. From there it flows northward to Orléans, and then turns westward to reach the Atlantic at St. Nazaire.

The Loire's flow is extremely irregular, with eight times more water in December and January than in August and September. The river is only partly navigable. It is linked both to the Saône and to the Seine by canals. Near its mouth another canal enables barges to sail safely from the Loire city of Nantes to the Breton seaport of Brest, without venturing out into the Atlantic.

PRIDE OF THE LOIRE VALLEY. *The magnificent chateau of Chenonceaux was built in 1521. It is now the most popular of the many beautiful castles that dot the valley of the Loire river.* Courtesy of French Government Tourist Office

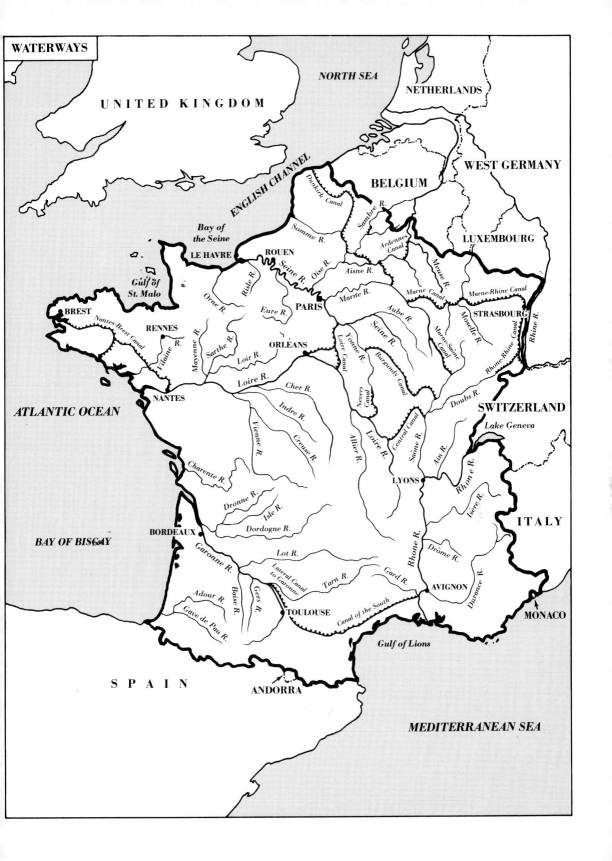

2. The Seine River

Second longest at 485 miles (780 kilometers) is the Seine. It rises in eastern France, runs westward through Paris and Rouen, and reaches the Atlantic at Le Havre. It is navigable throughout. Some of the longest canals in France have been constructed to extend the Seine's tributaries all the way east to the Rhine.

3. The Rhone River

The Rhone is actually 500 miles (800 kilometers) long but flows in France for only 324 miles (518 kilometers). Originating in Switzerland, it flows south from Lake Geneva and then west to a point just above the city of Lyons, where it converges with the Saône. From there it heads due south to form a reedy, marshy delta and then empties into the Mediterranean. The Rhone's tributaries bring the snowmelt from the Alps.

The river is navigable, partly because of the huge dams that have brought its swift-flowing waters under control at several points. It is the most industrially developed river in France.

A series of canals makes it possible to sail directly from a point on the Rhone just above Arles up into the Garonne. Still another canal links the Rhone to the Rhine.

4. The Garonne River

France's shortest principal river is the Garonne. It begins its 357-mile (575-kilometer) run in the Pyrenees and flows northwestward across the Aquitaine Basin to empty into the Atlantic above Bordeaux.

The country's first canal, built in the seventeenth century, connects the Garonne with the Mediterranean. That canal is now linked to others that extend the Garonne across the French southland to the Rhone.

5. The Rhine River

The heavily traveled Rhine is Europe's second most important river after the Danube. But it touches France only at Alsace, where it forms a 125-mile (200-kilometer) natural border with West Germany. Two major tributaries, the Moselle and the Meuse, flow into it from the eastern Paris Basin. Canals from the Seine and the Rhone provide waterborne access to the Rhine from inside France.

Forests

France possesses the largest forests in western Europe. Covering 54,000 square miles (14 million hectares), they comprise nearly half the forest lands of all the countries in the European Economic Community.

In ancient times, the forests may have covered 60 percent of the territory. Later they were ruthlessly exploited. By the time of the French Revolution (1789–1799), only about 23,000 square miles (6 million hectares) remained. Since then, conservation and reforestation programs have more than made up the losses.

Nature has endowed France with a land well suited to richly productive agriculture. But the country possesses relatively few of the resources needed for industry. The hardworking and ingenious French people have nevertheless found ways to use what they have—and to import what they need—in order to develop an economy that ranks among the world's most advanced.

CHAPTER IX

The People

The people of France have lived through a turbulent history. They have made the most of their fertile, varied land and have developed unique ways of life adapted to it. But what kind of people have they become? How are they meeting the challenges of a changing world?

They are a people that is changing today more rapidly and in more complex ways than ever before. Yet there are certain deep-rooted qualities and characteristics that have persisted through all the upheavals their country has seen. Whether one considers their class relationships, their religious affiliations, their population problem, or their health, the overall impression that emerges is one of ceaseless renewal within an underlying framework of stability.

A Matter of Class

Despite revolutions and reforms, the class structure of France remains surprisingly rigid. Of the 2,500 most famous or most powerful people in France today, only 3 percent were brought up in working-class homes.

The one class that has experienced the most drastic change is the old aristocracy. It dominated the country and set the standards in manners and customs until well into the nineteenth century. But its wealth was largely based on landed property. That form of wealth has been eroded by inflation, ever-increasing taxes, and loss of political power.

WOMEN ON STRIKE. *Workers in Champagne demonstrate to protest low wages and poor working conditions in the munitions factories. Women have historically played a major role in the French labor movement.* Culver Pictures

These aristocrats once scorned the very idea of working for a living. Over the past 150 years many of them have accepted high-level jobs in banking, industry, and business. They have tended to merge, often by marriage, with those who own or manage the bigger businesses. This is the group known as the upper bourgeoisie.

The bourgeoisie holds nearly all the top-salaried jobs. It is practically guaranteed these positions because it dominates the universities and the elite schools—the famous *grandes écoles*—that provide the necessary specialized training.

For those over sixteen years of age, French education is more rigidly divided along class lines than in some other western countries. Less than 10 percent of all university students come from workers' homes. That is even fewer than in Great Britain, a country notorious for its age-old class distinctions.

France has a middle class, but it has traditionally been comparatively small. It is, however, growing fast these days.

The most stubborn gap is that between the workers and the bourgeoisie. Contact between them is minimal. The bourgeoisie generally keeps itself aloof from the lives, interests, and problems of those who work for them.

Yet in some ways, as the workers' wages and living standards have risen, the two classes have increasingly shared the same life-styles. The more highly paid skilled workers may drive the same cars, wear the same leisure clothes, watch the same television programs, even spend their vacations in similar ways as the upper class.

The average French worker's purchasing power has risen by nearly 200 percent since 1950. By the early 1980s his average monthly wage was F 2,380 (a little under $400). That is not exactly great wealth, but it is considerably better than the low wage levels of the 1940s and 1950s. It contrasts sharply, however, with the average monthly income of chief executives of French corporations: F 87,083 ($14,514).

The upper classes are not only incomparably richer but hold on to more of their wealth. The principal method is said to be tax evasion. Businessmen and professionals often get away with disclosing only a small part of their incomes. The government simply lacks the staff to collect.

It is also true that most French government offices are staffed by individuals largely drawn from the bourgeoisie. They tend not to be overly zealous about prosecuting tax evaders of the same social class.

Wage earners get about 55 percent of all earned income, but they pay 84 percent of all income taxes. They are also hit harder by other kinds of taxes.

American wage earners pay a considerably smaller share of total income taxes, with corporations paying a proportionally higher share. The United States, too, has its tax evaders, but they are far fewer than in France. Would-be evaders know the risk of detection and prosecution is high in this country.

A recent report by a leading European economic organization showed that in France the top 10 percent of the people received over 30 percent of all net income. The bottom 20 percent got 6.5 percent. This is the biggest class differential in western Europe.

In these circumstances, friction between workers and capitalists has been inevitable. We have seen how it escalated into revolutionary violence on several occasions in the nineteenth century. It also produced radical socialist and anarchist movements.

The twentieth century has seen the birth of the French Communist Party. Its power and influence peaked in the years following World War II. The Party was often able to amass popular votes exceeding 25 percent of the total. It elected impressive numbers of deputies and senators to the Parliament, along with many local officials. Communist strength has waned considerably since then, but the Party remains a force to be reckoned with.

Governments of the 1970s and 1980s have attempted a variety of measures to close the gap and redistribute the wealth. Some of these measures hit the rich quite hard. One result so far has been considerable smuggling of capital and other valuables to foreign countries.

The single factor that has eased the situation for the workers is a remarkable rise in living standards in recent years. Nearly all French wage earners have benefited.

The People's Religions

Approximately 80 percent of the French consider themselves Roman Catholics. The figure is deceptive, however. Only about one in five of these attends church regularly. The majority attends services only on major occasions, such as baptisms, first communions, marriages, and deaths. Some parts of the country are so irreligious that the Church regards them as territories requiring the attention of missionaries. Recruitment of priests and nuns has become difficult.

The decline of French Catholicism has a long history. By the eighteenth century, the Church was by far the largest landowner in France. Its highest prelates were drawn from the most important aristocratic families. Many lived lives of luxury and conspicuous extravagance, while they themselves were exempt from taxation. High churchmen exercised considerable influence in determining the way the country was governed.

Inevitably, the Church's wealth and power incurred the resentment of the common people. We have seen how the Church became one of the principal targets of the Revolution of 1789, with its property seized and its priests subjected to government supervision. Anticlericalism persisted as a major factor in all the revolutionary upheavals of the nineteenth century. It remains an influential force in French life today.

In an attempt to confront today's realities, the French Church has

MIRACULOUS GROTTO. *Worshippers from many parts of the world pray at the shrine of Lourdes in southeastern France, where visions of the Virgin Mary appeared to a young peasant girl. The grotto's spring waters are believed to have miraculous healing powers.*
French Cultural Services/Universal Photos

adopted liberal views on political and social issues. It has also sought to develop interfaith relations with other religious groups.

The Protestant minority numbers about 800,000. Its members have long played a special role in French society. They occupy a disproportionately high number of important positions in government, business, and the professions. Groupings of them can be found in eastern France (in Alsace and the Jura), in south central France, and along the central region of the Atlantic coast.

Half of France's 700,000 Jews reside in the Paris area, with another quarter in Marseilles. The remainder live mostly in the eastern regions. Some have achieved eminence in banking, business, the professions, and the arts. A majority of French Jews is middle class, with a smaller but substantial number in the working class.

The Muslim community comprises mostly the million and a half Arab immigrants from the former French colonies of Algeria, Morocco, and Tunisia. Most are recent arrivals. Their distinctive religion is perceived as an alien import by the French. Hence it is one of several factors that tend to hinder the Muslims' acceptance into French society.

Needed: A Population Explosion

Nearly 300 years ago, France was the most densely populated country in Europe. The first census was attempted in 1707. It indicated that the population was about 19 million (modern experts have recently corrected this to 21 million).

By 1850 the nation had grown to about 36 million. In comparison, Britain's population (excluding Ireland) in 1800 was only 10 million. It had doubled by 1850 but was still substantially lower than that of France.

But after 1850 the French growth rate slowed drastically. The total did not reach 40 million until 1910. By that time, the British had topped the French with over 45 million. More dangerously, Germany had attained the alarming figure of 63 million.

This slowdown in French population development had several causes. The French may have been the first European nation to use birth control, starting at the time of the Revolution. Laws passed in that era required that all children were entitled to equal shares in the family inheritance. One result was that bourgeois parents began to limit the number of their children, producing an average of only two or three. The decline took place despite advances in medical science that reduced the death rate significantly during the nineteenth and early twentieth centuries. Life expectancy had actually doubled. But there was a virtual collapse of the birthrate. It plummeted from forty births per 1,000 people in the mid-1800s to a shockingly low 14.6 in 1939.

There were several reasons. France suffered incredibly in World War I, losing about 1½ million young men out of a total population of 41 million. The effects on the birthrate over the next several decades were disastrous.

Then came the 1930s, years of economic crisis and depression. Millions were unemployed. Many couples viewed the prospect of raising children as a hardship rather than a joy. There were some years during this grim period when there were more deaths than births in France, with the population actually declining. In an effort to halt the decline, the government passed strict laws against abortion and banned the sale and use of contraceptives. These laws were not repealed until the 1980s.

The depression had not ended when World War II broke out in 1939. Germany, with a population swollen to nearly 70 million, was able to put twice as many men into uniform as France. The French army was quickly overwhelmed. France surrendered to Germany in 1940. Relatively few Frenchmen were killed in the brief six weeks of major combat, but millions of French soldiers were held in prisoner-of-war camps till the war ended. Again, the birthrate dropped sharply.

At the war's end the men came home. Their return brought on the biggest *bébé-boom* ("baby boom") in French history. From 1946 to 1968, France added 10 million new citizens to its population. It had taken 135 years to add the previous 10 million. By the late 1960s there were twice as many youngsters under twenty-five as there had been at the start of World War II—a hopeful sign for the future.

The population had totaled only 41 million in 1946. Today it exceeds 55½ million. A major factor contributing to this expansion was a high rate of immigration in the postwar years.

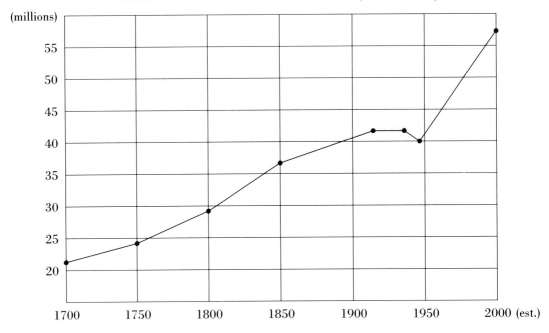

POPULATION TRENDS IN MODERN FRANCE (1700–2000)

Though the birthrate has again declined since the mid-1970s, France still has one of the highest in Europe. This is partly due to the fact that the proportion of the population under twenty-five is still comparatively high, at 28.5 percent. The highest birthrates are to be found among the immigrants.

There were more than 12 million French families in the late 1980s. Nearly 750,000 were headed by a single parent. The vast majority of these were women.

As in many western countries, where the number of children in each family has been dropping for some years, the size of the French household has been shrinking steadily. In 1861 there were an average of 3.84 people in each home. Today the average is 2.70. That means less than one child per home.

On the plus side, the population figures also reflect one of the world's lowest rates of infant mortality: of every 1,000 babies born, only fifteen die during their first year. Recent advances in medical science and the increased availability of excellent government-subsidized medical care have produced this good result. It helps explain why France is growing at an average net rate of 200,000 people each year.

The overall picture gives grounds for hope but also for pessimism. With so many young people, France can look forward to years of dynamism, creativity, and growth. But the country's ultimate destiny will inevitably depend on the birthrate—a statistic that has risen for only brief periods in recent history.

The nation also includes a high proportion of elderly people. About 14 percent of the population is over sixty-five, and the number is rising.

The People's Health

The life expectancy of the French has risen sharply in this century. Frenchmen today can expect to live an average of seventy years, while women average eight additional years. These figures match those of Americans exactly.

Among causes of death, heart ailments and cancers are the leading killers. Frenchmen are especially vulnerable to lung and throat cancer, mainly because they tend to smoke and drink heavily.

With 4 million alcoholics—about one person in fourteen—France holds the world record. Alcoholism is among the top causes of death, although the number of victims has declined slightly in recent years. In 1964 the average adult was consuming 132 quarts (120 liters) of wine per year. Today the average is down to 90 quarts (82 liters). But among alcohol users, 12 percent drink more than a quart a day.

French women drink three and a half times less than men and die of alcoholism four to five times less often.

The relatively new menace of Acquired Immune Deficiency Syndrome (AIDS) is looming ever larger in France. AIDS is a viral infection transmitted either sexually or through the use of infected hypodermic syringes. It attacks the body's immune defenses, leaving the victim vulnerable to many types of infection.

Recent years have witnessed the rapid spread of the AIDS epidemic through several parts of the world. The death rate is nearly 100 percent, as neither a preventive nor a cure has yet been found.

According to a recent article in *Le Monde*, authorities project there will be 21,000 AIDS cases in France by 1989. Estimates of the number of carriers of the virus who have not yet shown symptoms run as high as 200,000 persons. The government launched an extensive program of information and preventive measures in 1986.

A recent poll showed that one in four French persons worries about contracting AIDS. Yet only 17 percent have modified their sexual behavior. A massive 74 percent favors the sale of condoms in high schools and universities as a preventive measure.

Like young people elsewhere, French youngsters have developed special problems of their own. The fifteen-to-twenty-four age group now suffers well over 40 percent of all auto-accident deaths. This is western Europe's highest rate. It is the number-one cause of death among French youth.

Even more disturbing is the suicide rate among youngsters. It has doubled since the 1960s. Today an average of 1,000 youthful suicides is reported every year, with 40,000 unsuccessful attempts. Girls try suicide three times as often as boys, but boys succeed more often. Boys account for two thirds of these deaths.

Suicide is the second-highest cause of death among the young, after car accidents. Suspected reasons include the breakdown of family life, the rising divorce rate, the extreme competitiveness of the French educational system, economic problems, and a high rate of unemployment. But no direct cause-and-effect relationship has ever been proved. Complex emotional problems and other hidden motives undoubtedly play an important part.

French youngsters have been less involved in drug abuse than those of other western countries. Marijuana and hard drugs were relatively little used before 1970. Perhaps 7 percent have begun to use marijuana since then. The number of drug overdoses ranges from about 100 to 150 a year—one third the rate in neighboring West Germany, for example, and well below the rate in the United States.

In Paris, first-time drug offenders are allowed to choose medical treatment and rehabilitation instead of going to jail. If they stay "clean" for two years their arrest record is erased.

Still, the overall drug problem is worsening. Some 35,000 young people twelve to sixteen years old are believed to become addicted to heroin or cocaine each year. About 20,000 of these successfully complete rehabilitation programs.

Perhaps the most surprising fact about the French people is that none of their social, religious, medical, or demographic problems has hindered them from carrying out a near-miraculous transformation of their country's economy since the 1950s.

A Dynamic Economy

France is the world's fifth industrial power, after the United States, the U.S.S.R., Japan, and West Germany. Until about 1950, France had a reputation as a producer mainly of luxury goods, such as perfumes, fine wines, and high-fashion textiles and clothing. These French specialties are still in demand all over the world. But France today has developed into a world leader in advanced technology as well. French electronics and telecommunications equipment, automobiles and aircraft, chemical products and machinery are welcomed in many countries.

Early in the 1980s France drew even with Japan as one of the world's four leading exporters. Only the United States and West Germany export more.

The country's gross national product or GNP (the value of all goods and services produced) stood at F 782 billion ($130.3 billion) in 1970. It has since multiplied nearly six times, though a substantial part of the increase was due to inflation. The inflation rate peaked at about 13 percent in 1980; by the mid-1980s it had been brought below 5 percent. The GNP, which had been rising at a healthy 6.5 percent, was growing by only 2 percent in 1985 and has not improved much since then.

Natural Resources

The country's mineral and fuel resources are limited. Only coal, iron ore, bauxite, and uranium are relatively abundant. Deposits of petroleum, natural gas, and other metals are sparse.

The coalfields are in the north and northeast. They have been exploited for centuries. The seams of coal that still remain are extremely deep underground and are costly and difficult to extract. It is cheaper to import coal from abroad.

France was once among the world leaders in iron-ore production. The ore is extracted easily, but it is low-grade. Production has been dropping steadily in recent years. The government has backed the building of huge new steelmaking complexes on the coasts, at Dunkirk on the Channel and at Fos on the Mediterranean. These provide convenient access to imports of high-grade iron ore.

Bauxite is the ore from which aluminum is made. It is named after the southern French town of Les Baux, where it was discovered and where it has been mined for over a hundred years. Only one mine is still working today.

Sizable uranium deposits are mined in the Massif Central and in the west. They yield a plentiful 2,000 tons a year. Uranium is the main fuel for nuclear energy and weapons. In the years since World War II,

France has developed into the world's second-largest producer of nuclear energy for electricity (the United States is first). A government-owned company, Electricité de France, carries out virtually all production in this field.

Having its own domestic sources of nuclear fuel lessens France's dependence on imported fuel, especially oil. Foreign supplies of oil are expensive and can be cut off by the countries that control them.

By building more nuclear-power plants and using its own uranium to fuel them, Electricité de France plans to reduce oil imports to a minimum. Oil supplied nearly 60 percent of French energy in the early 1970s. Today nuclear power provides over 70 percent.

France has forty-three nuclear-power plants in operation. Only the United States with ninety-three and the U.S.S.R. with fifty-one have more. Nineteen more French plants are under construction.

France already has a surplus of nuclear power and sells about 8 percent to its neighbors. It also exports nuclear reactors and parts, along with French experts to set them up and help operate them.

But domestic demand keeps growing too. Consumption of electricity has risen by as much as 5 percent annually in recent years.

France does have some oil of its own, but only enough to supply 4 percent of its energy requirements. Over half the oil is found in the Paris Basin, with the rest mostly in the Landes region of the Aquitaine. Additional reserves were discovered under the North Sea, off the northwest coast, in the early 1970s. These are not expected to last beyond the year 2000.

The French have erected huge oil refineries at strategic seaport locations. They supply the country's petrochemical industries as well as

SUPER-GENERATOR. *Super Phenix, the world's most powerful nuclear generator, produces more fuel than it consumes. It went on line, feeding into the national electric power grid, in January 1986. Shown here is its core.* Courtesy of French Government Tourist Office

its energy needs. France does all its own oil refining.

The rivers provide another abundant source of electric power. Back in the late 1940s, the government launched a tremendous program of building hydroelectric dams. More than thirty dams have been constructed, taking advantage of practically every usable site. Hydroelectric power provides about 8 percent of France's needs.

French engineers have carried out a successful experiment in energy production at Rance, on the Breton coast. A specially designed power plant—the only one of its kind in the world—converts the energy of the tides into millions of watts of electricity.

France is also in the forefront of experimentation with solar energy. Europe's first solar furnace was erected in the western Pyrenees, the country's sunniest area, in 1970. It was for test purposes only. So successful was it that a much larger one has been built nearby, which produces 3 megawatts (3 million watts) of electricity.

SOLAR FACTORY. *The Pernod factory complex in Lyons derives a large part of its electricity from solar energy. It has no chimneys and emits no polluting waste matter. Pernod is one of France's largest producers of alcoholic beverages.* Courtesy of French Government Tourist Office

Huge reserves of natural gas were discovered at Lacq, close to the Pyrenees, in 1951. They still supply about one third of French gas consumption. The rest is imported.

Agriculture

France's agricultural resources consist of fertile farmlands, extensive forests, and of course farmers. About one third of the entire territory is suitable for farming. The forests cover about a quarter.

French farming has undergone revolutionary changes in the past several decades. It was once dominated by small family farms. As late as 1970, half of all the farms were less than 30 acres (12 hectares). Productivity and standards of living were low. Most of these small holdings have since been grouped into larger and more efficient enterprises.

One method of improving efficiency has been a government-backed policy known as *remembrement* ("consolidation"). For reasons reaching far back into history, many farms consisted of widely separated strips of land. Since the mid-1940s the government has encouraged farmers to swap parcels of land so that the farms could be consolidated. Nearly 30 million acres (12 million hectares) have been exchanged under this program. French farms now average about 69 acres (28 hectares).

The farm population has been dropping steadily, as it has in most industrialized nations. Farming engaged 35 percent of the French working population in 1939; today the amount has dropped to about 8 percent. An estimated 6 million people have left the farms since World War II. The farm population is expected to stabilize at about 5 to 6 percent.

Yet farm productivity is now six times greater than it was in 1946. This surprising result has been achieved by three means. First, small farms have been consolidated into larger, more efficient properties. Second, the machine has triumphed on the French farm. Old-fashioned methods have been abandoned in favor of modern techniques. As one example, French farmers today own an impressive 1½ million tractors. Third, French farmers have learned the advantages of large-scale cooperatives. Co-ops have existed in France for at least eighty years, but they have expanded tenfold since 1970.

In some of these co-ops, farmers pool their labor, equipment, and marketing facilities. In others, they share the cost of purchasing or renting the heavier, more expensive types of equipment. Other co-ops pool farmers' funds for investment in irrigation systems or electrification.

A few specialized co-ops have been set up to compete with big multinational food-processing companies. The government actively assists such co-ops, in order to limit foreign invasions of the French economy. One of them, the Conserveries Gard, started by local farmers, now ranks among Europe's biggest and most successful.

Wheat, barley, and oats are the main cereal crops that provide surpluses for export. Sugar derived from sugar beets is another major food export. Fruit, potatoes, and vegetables are also grown on a big scale.

About half of France's extensive cattle herds are used for dairy products. The rest supply beef, for both domestic and foreign consumption.

France does need to import certain foodstuffs, notably meats and processed foods. But in recent years its agricultural exports have usually topped its imports.

CHEESE FOR THE WORLD. *Workers in a cave in the tiny village of Roquefort-sur-Soulzon prepare famous, tangy Roquefort cheese for world markets.* Courtesy of French Embassy, Press and Information Division

FEATHERED HARVEST. *Farmers in the Herbihan region, Brittany, gather turkeys to prepare them for market.* Photo by Guy Le Querrec; Copyright Magnum Photos

Only Italy grows more wine grapes than France. Over 2.47 million acres (1 million hectares) are devoted to the French crop. Wine production currently totals around 1,848 million gallons (70 million hectoliters).

French wines fall into two broad categories: the more expensive fine wines, sometimes called the "noble" wines, and the ordinary table wines. The first type includes such well-known vintages as Burgundy, Bordeaux, Champagne, and Beaujolais. All such wines are carefully classified in four levels of quality, identified on the labels.

The *vins ordinaires* ("ordinary wines") amount to over two thirds the total. Grown almost entirely by small farmers in the southeastern region called Languedoc, nearly all are consumed in France. The French drink more wine than any other nationality.

Cheap Italian and Spanish imports are giving the producers of *vin ordinaire* tough competition. In good wine-growing years, when there is a bumper crop, more of this wine is produced than can be sold. In the 1960s the government introduced a new policy of encouraging the growers to uproot their poorer vines and replace them with "noble" ones. The better wines are suitable for export and hence are easier to market.

Commercial use of France's vast forests is closely supervised by the government. At a time when wood is becoming a rare commodity in other countries, French forests are actually expanding. Their timber provides the raw material for buildings, furniture, and papermaking. These industries employ some 650,000 people in 100,000 enterprises.

French agriculture has benefited from the establishment of a West European Common Market for farm goods in the late 1950s. Its twelve member countries agreed to admit each other's products without tariffs or quotas. With this guaranteed market, French farmers have substantially increased their production for export.

The Industrial Miracle

French industry, too, has experienced a virtual revolution over the past half century. In the 1930s and 1940s it was technically backward and production was shrinking. Most enterprises employed fewer than ten workers.

Modernization and expansion began in the early 1950s. Production had tripled within twenty years.

Since then French industry has transformed itself—and transformed French society at the same time. Huge factory complexes using the latest computerized controls, robots, and other technological innovations have replaced many of the old small-scale workshops. New employment opportunities have attracted millions from the farms and villages. A quarter of the working population labors in manufacturing, and twice as many in the service industries.

The pacesetter has been the aerospace industry. France has a long tradition as a pioneer in airplane design and manufacture. In 1970 government financing backed the establishment of a giant new international consortium, Airbus Industries. It is French led, though the French government and a West German firm each own 38 percent. Lesser shares are owned by British, Dutch, Belgian, and Spanish companies. Aircraft components are built in all these countries and assembled in Toulouse, France's aerospace headquarters. Airbus is the most successful aircraft manufacturer in Europe.

The French industry started from a difficult position. In the years just after World War II, the United States controlled 90 percent of the world's commercial aircraft production (it still has 80 percent). The first French response came in 1952 with a fast, medium-range passenger plane, the Caravelle. Nearly 300 were sold to thirty-four airlines within the next twenty years.

Unfortunately, the French and British governments then joined in a strategic error. Instead of building a new plane that improved on the Caravelle, they gambled that the future lay in supersonic (faster than the speed of sound) air travel. Together they invested heavily in creating the world's first supersonic passenger jet, the Concorde. Few were sold. Concorde flights are still maintained on some air routes, but the sleek, needle-nosed plane has never earned the hoped-for rich profits.

Since then the Airbus company has sponsored production of a series of subsonic jets. These fast, efficient, medium-range planes have been so popular with airlines all over the world that at some points orders were being received faster than they could be filled.

Another French company, Aérospatiale, does most of the actual plane building for Airbus. It is also the world's third-largest manufacturer of helicopters. Its choppers have even penetrated the American market, where the competition is fierce. This company is entirely owned by the French government.

Air forces of many countries have chosen France's highly sophisticated Mystère and Mirage jet fighters. The new twinjet Mirage 2000, capable of flying at Mach 2.5 (two and a half times the speed of sound), is racking up record sales. Plans are already under way for a successor, the Rafale, to be operational by 1996.

Another French firm, SNECMA, works with General Electric in manufacturing airplane engines. One family of its engines, the CFM 56, has been incorporated into the latest models of the Boeing 737 and the new Airbus A-320.

The industry was recently earning a gross annual income of over F 50 billion ($8.3 billion). Nearly two thirds of its production was for export. Half the exports were civil aircraft and half were military.

A large part of the export military aircraft were sold to Third World countries. With the planes went rapidly increasing quantities of other weapons. Total arms sales to these countries more than quadrupled in a single recent year. France has become the second-biggest arms supplier to the Third World after the U.S.S.R., with 28.2 percent of the total.

Substantial quantities of French weapons go to the United States and western Europe. Tactical missiles—the Exocet, the Magic, and the Roland—are the biggest sellers.

The automobile industry, too, was a success story until about 1980. Many of its factories had been badly damaged or destroyed during World War II, but it rose out of the ashes to become the world's fourth-biggest producer by the 1950s. Autos led all other French exports. Total sales were slightly below the record-breaking sales of West Germany but well ahead of Italy's and Britain's.

The smaller French family cars with low gas consumption have been especially popular both inside France and abroad. The average French family spends about one seventh of its budget on cars and uses them for 80 percent of all trips.

By the mid-1980s France was producing over 3 million cars a year. About half were exported. Production was concentrated in two giant firms: state-owned Renault and the recently merged Peugeot–Citroën. They are the largest auto companies in Europe and among the six largest in the world. Renault earned a profit of over a billion francs ($167 million) in 1979 but then experienced some bad years. Sales rebounded in 1987, and profits soared to new records of between 2 and 3 billion francs ($333 to $500 million).

The two companies have recently started joint enterprises with foreign firms, such as Italy's Fiat and automakers in South America. Citroën has even set up an auto factory in Rumania, a communist country.

The Workers

About one fourth of French labor is unionized. This is a considerably lower percentage than is found in other west European countries.

The largest group of unions is the Confédération Générale du Travail (General Federation of Labor). Its membership is estimated at about 1.2 million, though it claims many more. It has strong ties to the Communist Party.

The CGT's main rival is the Confédération Française Démocratique du Travail (French Democratic Federation of Labor). This Socialist group has about 900,000 members. About the same size is the Force Ouvrière (Workers' Force), a reformist body that tends to cooperate with management.

ROBOTS ON THE LINE. *High technology has triumphed in French factories. Here a Renault automobile assembly line is serviced by computerized robots.* Courtesy of French Government Tourist Office

These splits make united labor action difficult. From 1968 to 1987, there were less than half as many strikes in France as in the United States. French workers seemed to prefer one-day nationwide work stoppages.

One successful technique for increasing efficiency and reducing labor unrest was developed at the big Aérospatiale helicopter plant near Marseilles. The 6,500 workers were divided into semiautonomous groups. Each was responsible for one phase of the assembly process. The group could schedule its own time. Working hours were flexible within a framework of forty-one half-hour slots running between 6:30 A.M. and 6:30 P.M. To reduce boredom, workers were encouraged to learn several trades and move from one shop to another.

Nearly 10,000 other companies have since adopted similar methods. Some even have a forty-hour week set up on a four-day schedule. The result has been a significant gain in worker satisfaction and productivity and a reduction in stoppages and strikes.

The legal minimum wage is linked to the cost of living, an important factor in view of France's long record of inflation. The inflation rate peaked at 13 percent in 1980, fell to 5 percent by 1985, and has fluctuated since then.

Despite economic growth, unemployment has grown into a stubborn and worsening problem. It affected only 4 percent of the working population in 1976, but then it climbed to a painful 13 percent in the mid-1980s. About 2.5 million were out of work, including a large percentage of young workers under twenty-five. The problem is generally thought to be structural (that is, built into the economic system). It also reflects the depressed conditions that have recently affected world trade. A wide range of remedies has been proposed. Government planners have devoted special attention to creating jobs for the young.

Foreign Trade

The most important factor affecting France's trade with other countries was the formation of the European Community, or Common Market, in 1957. Its original membership of six west European countries made a historic agreement to eliminate tariffs and quotas and encourage free trade. The Common Market now has twelve members. Together they form France's biggest trading partner, buying nearly half its exports and selling it more than half its imports. Within the Common Market, West Germany is France's biggest single customer, then Italy, then Belgium and Luxembourg, and then Britain.

In recent years France has been the eighth-largest exporter to the United States, delivering 2.5 percent of all American imports. The United States is the third-largest exporter to France.

French wines, brandies, and liqueurs do especially well in the United States. But the country's exports to the United States also include a much larger high-tech component: automobiles and spare parts, airplanes and helicopters, plane engines and parts, steel products, electronic and telecommunications equipment, and chemicals. The United States sells France mainly computers and electronic-information equipment, plane engines, control and regulation equipment, semiconductors, chemicals, and coal.

French investors have a sizable stake in the United States. It totals over F 30 billion ($5 billion). The French would like to invest even more. Their experts have carried out detailed analyses of the American market.

One such study advises French businessmen hoping to open branches in the United States to consult knowledgeable Americans. They must make sure that their products and the way in which they are presented are well adapted to American tastes. The study warns of the American "consumer king," who "comparison shops, expects discounts, changes his mind, and returns merchandise—even articles of the highest luxury class!"

Like other advanced countries, France is a big exporter of investment capital as well as goods. She ranks fifth in this field, with one year's investments in foreign countries totaling F 248 billion ($41.3 billion). Most of these funds go to former French colonies and other underdeveloped countries.

Road, Rail, and Air Transportation

With so much of the nation's economic, political, and cultural life centered in Paris, it was inevitable that the road and rail networks would radiate from the capital city. This pattern often made it difficult to travel directly among the other cities and regions. New roads and rail lines have been built, and more are under construction, to remedy the problem.

In 1960 France had less than 72 miles (120 kilometers) of *autoroutes* ("superhighways"). Today, there are nearly 4,200 miles (7,000 kilometers) of these and nearly 18,000 miles (30,000 kilometers) of first-class *routes nationales* ("national roads"), plus extensive systems of local and rural roadways. The French highway network is the densest in western Europe.

The country's railways employ sophisticated technology that in some instances surpasses the finest available in any other country. With about 21,000 miles (35,000 kilometers) of track, they carry 750 million passengers in an average year. One third of the system is electrified, cutting fuel costs and pollution.

French railway equipment and know-how are exported to many parts of the world. The French industry recently won out over rivals in several

TGV. *The* Train à Grande Vitesse *("High Speed Train") set an as yet unbeaten world speed record of 228 mph (380 kph) in 1981. Its regular speed when carrying passengers is 162 mph (270 kph).* Courtesy of French Embassy, Press and Information Division

countries to land enormous contracts for equipment sales to China, Zaire, and several U.S. cities.

The first subway system ever built in the Middle East and Africa opened in Cairo, Egypt, in September 1987. Financed by French low-interest loans and constructed jointly by France and Egypt, the 27-mile (43-kilometer), $300-million line featured state-of-the-art French equipment.

On February 26, 1981, a new kind of train established a world speed record that still stands unchallenged. This was France's *train à grande vitesse* or TGV ("high-speed train"). It zoomed along at 228 miles (380 kilometers) per hour. A special track had been constructed for it on the Paris–Lyons line, one of the country's most heavily traveled routes.

TGVs now run routinely and safely on this and other lines at an average speed of 162 miles (270 kilometers) per hour. Each carries about 375 passengers. The TGV system is steadily expanding to other French cities and to connect with the Belgian, Dutch, West German, and Spanish railways—and even the British, through the new tunnel under the English Channel.

Two large firms dominate the country's air-transport industry. Air France has a near monopoly on international air travel. It carries about 12 million passengers to and from seventy-three countries each year. An international study of air safety in the mid-1980s ranked Air France as the world's second safest, after the Australian airline Qantas.

Inside France, Air Inter carries about 10 million passengers to thirty cities. Numerous smaller companies serve other domestic aviation needs.

French airports are the second busiest in Europe after those of Britain, serving some 30 million passengers a year. They handle more freight than any other European airports. About 800 commercial planes take off or land every day. Busiest of all are Paris's two great international airports, Orly and the newer Roissy–Charles-de-Gaulle.

Tourism

The biggest benefits from the recent improvements in transportation affect the tourist industry. It ranks first in profitability among all the service industries. Tourism currently brings the country over F 13 billion a year ($2.16 billion).

With about 55,500,000 visitors staying for extended periods, France shares with England the title of Europe's most popular destination. The largest number by far (over 15 million) come from West Germany. Britain is second with fewer than half as many, followed by Switzerland, Belgium, Holland, Italy, the United States, and Spain. Even far-off Japan sends nearly half a million tourists.

Telecommunications

The postal, telephone, and telecommunications systems are owned and operated by the government. They consume the second-largest share of the national budget (education is first), with approximately F 150 billion ($25 billion) a year.

The French telephone system was long notorious for unreliable equipment and service. A thorough reconstruction program under way since 1974 has transformed the system into one of the world's finest. The number of phone lines has more than tripled.

The French-produced Ariane rocket placed the Telecom I satellite in space in 1984. It was the first of several, meant to ensure the country an independent means of worldwide communication.

The government has also backed the development of the remarkable electronic-communications system known as Minitel. The system provides telephone subscribers with a computer terminal, installed in their homes at no extra charge. They can then use the computer to look up phone numbers, make plane or train reservations, order theater tickets, or communicate via electronic mail. There is even a service called "pink electronic mail," which provides a dating service. Users can access an astonishing total of 1,500 videotext services. Minitel has been made available to some 3 million users so far in France. This number is bound to increase rapidly, as the system is being made accessible to users in the United States. Users pay only each time they use the system.

The Minitel system is a small but dramatic example of the transformations that have reshaped French economic life. A country that was predominantly agricultural, technically backward, and relatively inactive in world markets became a formidable competitor, predominantly urban and industrialized, and impressively equipped for the world of tomorrow.

A Democratic Government

Feudalism; absolute monarchy; constitutional monarchy; empire; puppet government; democracy—in its long history, France has experienced all these forms of government.

Feudalism was a highly decentralized system. The feudal lords ran their fiefs with little or no interference from any central authority other than the church. But starting in the sixteenth century, except for a few brief periods, power was increasingly concentrated in the hands of France's monarchs.

Even with the final triumph of republican government as embodied in the democratic constitution of 1875, the national government still controlled the principal levers of power. Control of the economy received special attention.

The Economic Role of the State

For some 300 years, the government has played a larger role in the French economy than in that of most other western countries. This policy is known as *dirigisme* ("directionism") or *étatisme* ("statism"). The tradition dates back at least to King Louis XIV, who was the first ruler to take over a private enterprise (the tobacco industry).

Louis XIV was also the first to order a form of economic planning by government experts for the whole country. Around 1800, Napoleon developed a more elaborate planning system. Since World War II, a government agency known as the Commissariat for the Plan has laid out a series of five-year plans for the nation's economy. Its proposals are advisory rather than compulsory, but the government has ways of pressuring the various economic enterprises to carry out its policies.

Throughout the nineteenth century, the government invested public funds to promote the development of railways, banks, and heavy industry, and to improve French wines. In the mid-1930s, a government with socialistic leanings, called the Popular Front, nationalized most of the arms industry, the railways, and part of the Bank of France. It also set up state-run aeronautical firms. The postal, telephone, and telecommunications systems were already owned and operated by the government.

An even bigger wave of nationalizations took place after World War II. The state took over the Renault automobile company, Air France, the coal mines, the electric and gas companies, and the larger insurance companies. It acted partly because the managements of some of these companies had collaborated with the enemy occupation forces during the war.

The first serious steps toward decentralization were taken in 1972. A share of power was allotted to the twenty-two newly established

Governments of France
(1792–Present)

SPAN	NAME	MAJOR FIGURES
1792–1804	First Republic	Maximilien Robespierre, Georges Danton, Napoleon Bonaparte
1804–1815	First Empire	Emperor Napoleon I
1815–1830	Bourbon Restoration	King Louis XVIII, King Charles X
1830–1848	Orléans Monarchy	King Louis Philippe
1848–1852	Second Republic	Louis-Napoleon Bonaparte

regional governments. The ninety-six existing departments were also granted enlarged responsibilities.

The Socialist government elected in 1981 was ambivalent about decentralization. On the one hand it nationalized several big banks and other major industrial concerns, thereby strengthening government mastery of the economy. On the other hand the Socialists actively promoted the development of cultural institutions throughout the country.

Then came the conservatives' victory in the parliamentary election of 1986. They returned several of the nationalized firms to private owner-

SPAN	NAME	MAJOR FIGURES
1852–1871	Second Empire	Emperor Napoleon III
1871–1940	Third Republic	Adolphe Thiers, Jules Ferry, Georges Clemenceau, Léon Blum
1940–1944	Vichy Regime	Marshal Philippe Pétain
1940–1944	Free France	Charles de Gaulle
1944–1946	Provisional Government	Charles de Gaulle
1946–1958	Fourth Republic	Pierre Mendès-France
1958–present	Fifth Republic	Charles de Gaulle, François Mitterrand

ship. Whether to continue this trend toward "privatization" or to carry out even more nationalizations is the subject of a bitter debate between the left-wing political parties and those of the right wing. The debate is likely to rage on for the foreseeable future.

The Foundations of Government

France is a democratic republic. Like the United States, it is governed according to the principles set down in a written constitution. The first constitution was proclaimed in 1791, during the French Revolution.

Since then France has had eleven constitutions, each setting up a different form of monarchy or republican government. The constitution now in effect is that of the Fifth Republic, established in 1958.

As in all democracies, the people are the ultimate source of power. They express their will through free elections.

The French government is similar to that of the United States in that it has three separate branches: executive, legislative, and judicial. This "separation of powers" is designed to work as a system of checks and balances, in which each branch prevents any abuse of power by the others.

The United States also has three levels of government: national, state, and local. France has four: national, regional, departmental, and communal.

The National Government

The president of France is the chief of state. He is elected for a term of seven years by direct universal suffrage (the votes of all eligible men and women eighteen years of age or older). His principal task is to lay down the broad lines of national policy.

He appoints the prime minister, usually the leader of the party that controls the majority in Parliament. The prime minister acts as the head of government. There is no such office in the United States. The American President does the jobs that are done by both the president and prime minister in France.

The president of France also appoints all members of the Council of Ministers, as nominated by the prime minister. The council is similar to the U.S. President's cabinet.

As head of state, the president has primary responsibility for the shaping of foreign policy. Whenever there is a grave threat to the

The French System of Government

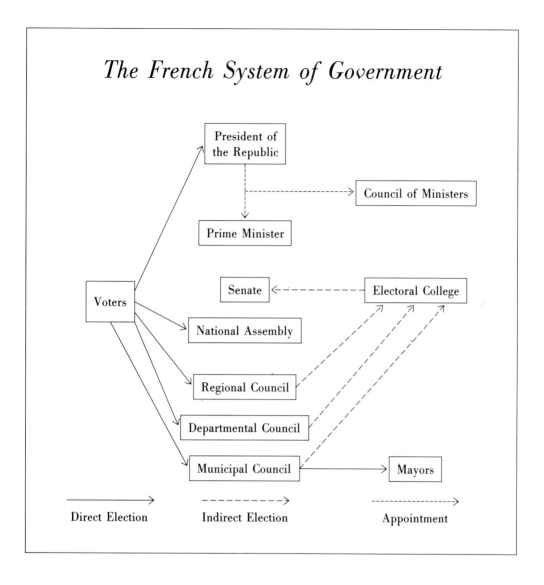

security of the nation, he may exercise extraordinary powers and rule by decree until safety and order have been restored.

No law passed by Parliament can go into effect unless it is approved and signed by the president. He has the power to dissolve Parliament at any time and to call for new elections, but he cannot do so more than once in any twelve-month period.

The prime minister is responsible for enforcement of the laws and the day-by-day running of the government. He supervises and coordinates the work of the ministers, who head the various agencies of the government. Under normal circumstances the prime minister is expected to carry out the broad policies set out by the president.

Working with his Council of Ministers, the prime minister develops proposals for new laws and government programs, which are then submitted to Parliament. If a majority of Parliament disapproves of the prime minister's proposals, it may pass a vote of censure or "no confidence." The prime minister and his ministers must then resign, and the president calls for new elections.

All this is spelled out in the constitution. It takes for granted that the president and the prime minister will be of the same party and will generally agree on matters of policy. But it does not specify what happens if the president and the prime minister are of opposing political parties. That happened for the first time after the 1986 elections. The country unexpectedly found itself with a Socialist president, François Mitterrand, and a conservative prime minister, Jacques Chirac.

The problem was resolved at least temporarily by "cohabitation." Under this informal arrangement, the two men agreed to remain in office and try to get along even though they disagreed about almost every political question of the day. Cohabitation ended after the 1988 presidential election, when Mitterrand defeated Chirac and replaced him with a Socialist prime minister.

The legislative power is vested in the Parliament. It consists of two houses, the National Assembly and the Senate. The 491 members of the Assembly are elected for five years by direct universal suffrage. The 322 senators are elected for nine years, through an indirect system in which local officials vote for an electoral college. Its sole function is to elect the senators. One third of the Senate comes up for election every three years.

All proposed laws originate in the National Assembly. The Senate can delay legislation but cannot propose any. To become law, bills have to be passed by both houses after they have agreed on the exact wording. If the two houses cannot reach agreement, the Assembly makes the final decision by itself. Parliament also has the exclusive power to authorize a declaration of war.

The Regional Governments

During the Revolution, the old provinces (Burgundy, Gascony, Picardy, etc.) were abolished. France was organized into ninety-six *départements* ("departments"). These worked fairly well for nearly 200 years, though many were hardly bigger than counties in the United States. Their borders were often arbitrary and artificial. More and more in recent times, the departments have proved an inefficient instrument for coping with the needs of modern life.

In 1972 the country was reorganized into twenty-two much larger administrative regions, each of which incorporated two to seven departments. Each region was formed out of an area that shared common natural features and economic interests.

Regional governments are empowered to act in many spheres. They have special authority to plan for economic development, promote cultural activities, and play an important part in education by building and equipping the *lycées* ("senior high schools"). The national government supplies the necessary funds.

Each region is governed by a Regional Council elected by direct universal suffrage. The council elects its own president, who serves as the region's chief executive.

The Departmental Governments

Under the former centralized system, each department used to be run by an all-powerful prefect appointed by the president. Today the departments elect their own general councils. These in turn elect a council president as chief executive. The former prefect has been renamed Commissioner of the Republic and the powers of the office reduced.

Departmental responsibilities range from social welfare to road and highway maintenance to building and maintenance of the *collèges* ("junior high schools").

In addition to the ninety-six departments of metropolitan France, five overseas departments have been created from former French colonies. The largest is French Guiana, on the northeast coast of South America. Next in size is Réunion, an island east of Madagascar in the Indian Ocean. The Caribbean islands of Martinique and Guadeloupe form two departments, while the tiny isles of St. Pierre and Miquelon, off the coast of Newfoundland, form a single one. The inhabitants of all five are French citizens, with the right to elect representatives to the Parliament in Paris.

Five other overseas territories, mostly islands in the Pacific, have not yet attained the status of departments. One of these, New Caledonia, has been the scene of a sometimes violent struggle between the native-born population and the French settlers. The former are demanding independence; the latter are insisting that the territory remain under French rule.

The Communal Governments

The basic units of government are the 36,000 communes. These include big cities such as Bordeaux and Lyons, as well as towns, villages, and

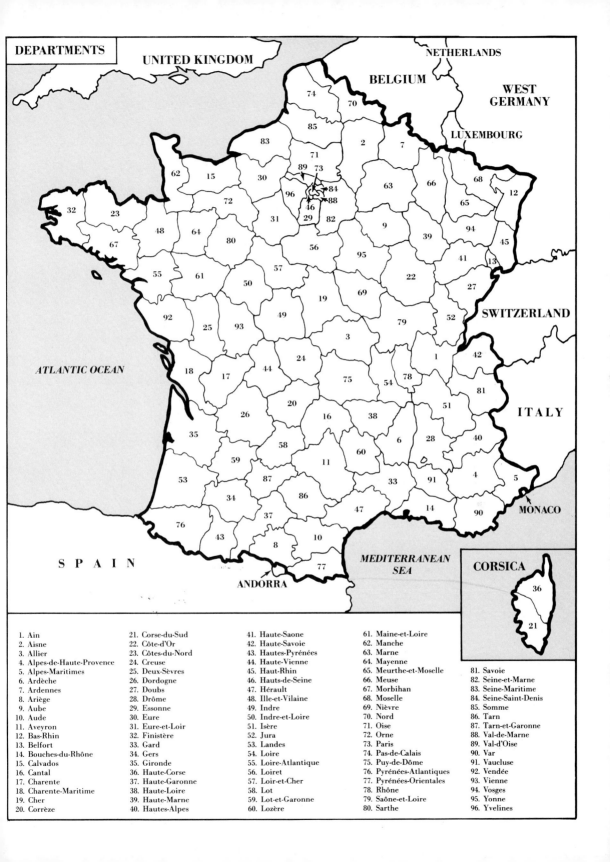

DEPARTMENTS

UNITED KINGDOM

NETHERLANDS

BELGIUM

WEST GERMANY

LUXEMBOURG

SWITZERLAND

ITALY

MONACO

ATLANTIC OCEAN

SPAIN

MEDITERRANEAN SEA

ANDORRA

CORSICA

1. Ain
2. Aisne
3. Allier
4. Alpes-de-Haute-Provence
5. Alpes-Maritimes
6. Ardèche
7. Ardennes
8. Ariège
9. Aube
10. Aude
11. Aveyron
12. Bas-Rhin
13. Belfort
14. Bouches-du-Rhône
15. Calvados
16. Cantal
17. Charente
18. Charente-Maritime
19. Cher
20. Corrèze

21. Corse-du-Sud
22. Côte-d'Or
23. Côtes-du-Nord
24. Creuse
25. Deux-Sèvres
26. Dordogne
27. Doubs
28. Drôme
29. Essonne
30. Eure
31. Eure-et-Loir
32. Finistère
33. Gard
34. Gers
35. Gironde
36. Haute-Corse
37. Haute-Garonne
38. Haute-Loire
39. Haute-Marne
40. Hautes-Alpes

41. Haute-Saone
42. Haute-Savoie
43. Hautes-Pyrénées
44. Haute-Vienne
45. Haut-Rhin
46. Hauts-de-Seine
47. Hérault
48. Ille-et-Vilaine
49. Indre
50. Indre-et-Loire
51. Isère
52. Jura
53. Landes
54. Loire
55. Loire-Atlantique
56. Loiret
57. Loir-et-Cher
58. Lot
59. Lot-et-Garonne
60. Lozère

61. Maine-et-Loire
62. Manche
63. Marne
64. Mayenne
65. Meurthe-et-Moselle
66. Meuse
67. Morbihan
68. Moselle
69. Nièvre
70. Nord
71. Oise
72. Orne
73. Paris
74. Pas-de-Calais
75. Puy-de-Dôme
76. Pyrénées-Atlantiques
77. Pyrénées-Orientales
78. Rhône
79. Saône-et-Loire
80. Sarthe

81. Savoie
82. Seine-et-Marne
83. Seine-Maritime
84. Seine-Saint-Denis
85. Somme
86. Tarn
87. Tarn-et-Garonne
88. Val-de-Marne
89. Val-d'Oise
90. Var
91. Vaucluse
92. Vendée
93. Vienne
94. Vosges
95. Yonne
96. Yvelines

in some cases districts within the larger municipalities.

Each commune is governed by a mayor and a municipal council, elected for six years by direct universal suffrage. They deal with economic and social matters affecting many aspects of the citizens' daily lives. Housing, zoning, provision of facilities for primary-school education, and protection of the environment are among their responsibilities.

The mayors have a special duty added to their normal ones. French law requires that all marriages be formalized in a civil ceremony, performed by the mayor or his deputy, before any religious ceremony may take place.

The Judicial System

French courts, like those in the United States, are independent of the legislative and executive branches of government. There are two types of courts. One deals with criminal cases and with civil cases between private persons. The other deals with lawsuits between individuals and public bodies.

Minor criminal offenses are tried in police and correctional courts. Courts of assize, which exist in every department, hear felony cases (serious offenses). Three judges preside in each court of assize; nine jurors render the verdicts. The death penalty was abolished in 1981.

Above these courts are the courts of appeals, which can review verdicts brought before them. The nation's highest court is the Cour de Cassation. It does not render final verdicts on individual cases as the U.S. Supreme Court does. Instead it interprets the law, and if it finds some legal flaw in a verdict, it can refer the case back to the lower courts.

Most of the 5,600 judges are graduates of the École Nationale de la Magistrature (National School for Magistrates), and all judges must pass a qualifying examination before they can be appointed. The French term *magistrat* covers both those who sit as trial judges *(magistrats de siège)* and those who serve as public prosecutors *(magistrats de parquet).*

The rights of persons accused of crime are protected by the Declaration of the Rights of Man, originally proclaimed in 1789 and restated in the constitution of 1958. The Declaration is similar in many ways to the U.S. Constitution's Bill of Rights.

An All-Encompassing Social Security System

The French people benefit from an extensive system of social welfare. Its chief purpose is to assist those in need, but it is also designed to narrow the persistent gap between upper- and lower-class incomes. More than one third of the income of the average household comes from government payments of one kind or another.

The principal benefits include old-age and retirement pensions, unemployment insurance, and health insurance. These have almost tripled since 1959, a rate faster than the rise in government revenues. The steep increases have been due at least partly to the lowering of the retirement age to sixty, the aging of the population, and mounting unemployment caused by the worldwide economic slowdown.

There are also many forms of family assistance. One allocation that is unknown in the United States is a monetary reward to mothers that rises with the number of children they have. Its purpose is to help raise the sagging birthrate.

Defense Forces: Small but Potent

Plans for the defense of France rely on both nuclear and conventional forces. The country's nuclear weapons include long-range missiles in silos, nuclear submarines armed with missiles, surface-to-surface tactical missiles, and Mirage IV bombers carrying ASMP missiles. France has an estimated 500 nuclear warheads.

The conventional forces comprise about 300,000 men and women in the army, 70,000 in the navy, and 100,000 in the air force. All Frenchmen eighteen years old or over are subject to one year's military or civil-defense service. Frenchwomen may volunteer for military duty.

France spends a little more than 4 percent of its gross national product on defense. The United States spends about 7 percent, Britain 5.3 percent, and West Germany 3.4 percent.

Though France is a member of NATO, it withdrew from the NATO unified military command in 1966. The purpose of this move was to ensure the country's full freedom of action. There is little doubt, however, that France would cooperate fully with the other democracies in the event of a major military threat to the security of the free world.

A Changing Educational System

No aspect of life in France has undergone more sweeping changes in recent years than education. Since 1968, a series of reforms has been attempted, aimed at making the school experience more democratic, more flexible, more practical, more closely geared to the job markets and other realities of life.

The earliest reform in education took place well over a century ago. Laws passed in 1881 and 1882 established a public education system that was free of charge, secular, and compulsory. Youngsters from six to thirteen were required to attend school. The minimum school-leaving age was later raised to fourteen, and in 1959 to sixteen. Prior to that time, the *lycées* received only a minority of junior high graduates. Now they had to accept much larger numbers.

About 13 million students were enrolled in primary and secondary education by the mid-1980s. That figure has varied widely before and since then, because the numbers in each age group have shifted.

In one fundamental way, French education differs radically from American. Virtually all schooling, from the primary schools through the universities, is under the jurisdiction of the Ministry of National Education. It designs the curriculum, chooses all books and materials, and hires the teachers. A few highly specialized institutions are governed by other ministries (agriculture, defense, culture, etc.), but these are still agencies of the national government.

Only the construction and equipment of the primary and secondary schools are left to the local communities. In the United States educational matters are controlled by the states, local communities, and often the local school districts.

In addition to the public system, French law allows for privately run schools. Almost all of these are Roman Catholic, with a tiny percentage of Protestant and Jewish schools. About 15 percent of all French youngsters attend the private schools. Not all do so for religious reasons; some of the private schools are thought to provide a superior education.

Most private schools are under contract to the state. It pays their teachers and provides nominal amounts to help cover the schools' expenses. In return the schools agree to follow the government curriculum.

Nursery and Primary Schools

A system of nursery schools developed only gradually over the past century. About 30 percent of two- to three-year-olds attend these schools today, but 90 percent of four- to five-year-olds do. French preschool teaching methods are famous for their flexible and innovative styles.

They are aimed at awakening the child's consciousness, giving practice in manual skills, and accustoming the child to group life. Children start learning to read at age five.

In the five-year primary schools, slower learners can be held back. Only half the students get through without repeating at least one year. Partly this is due to the high percentage of immigrant children. But it also reflects the French insistence on all children getting sound training in the fundamentals before being allowed to advance.

Secondary Schools

Students in *collèges* ("junior high schools") were grouped according to academic ability until 1975. That system was criticized as elitist and inefficient. Students of all ability levels are now grouped together in most classes. The new system does, however, provide supportive teaching for slow learners and advanced study for gifted students.

Training in computer skills has received steadily increasing emphasis of late. By 1988 the *collèges* had 100,000 microcomputers. Every student is required to spend at least thirty hours at the computer.

When students reach the age of fourteen, a decision must be made as to whether they should proceed to an academic *lycée,* enter a vocational *lycée,* or leave school to take prevocational or apprenticeship training. Until 1957 this crucial decision, which can determine a youngster's whole future, was based on an examination. Today parents, teachers, counselors, and administrators decide jointly with the student, after careful study of the student's academic record, aptitudes, and interests.

The system is not entirely impartial. Almost all of those recommended for the academic course are from the middle and upper classes.

The *lycées* offer a three-year curriculum. Some prepare students for an academic diploma known as the *baccalauréat.* Others provide techni-

COMPUTER KIDS. *Training in computer science is a regular feature of French education. Here, fascinated students at a* collège *("junior high school") receive instruction.* Courtesy of French Government Tourist Office

cal and vocational training. A little more than half the 2 million *lycéens* ("high school students") opt for the academic course.

American students would find life in these schools decidedly different from high school life as they know it. There is little afterschool or extracurricular activity, and no interschool sports competition.

Candidates for the *"bac"* or *"bachot,"* as the *baccalauréat* is familiarly called, take a highly competitive exam at the end of their studies. They may choose among several broad subject areas: philosophy and arts, economics and social sciences, mathematics and physical sciences, mathematics and life sciences, mathematics and technology.

About two thirds of the candidates pass the exam. Those who fail are ineligible for admission to the universities or other institutions of higher education. The pressures from parents, teachers, and others on youngsters taking the exam are probably even more intense than those on American high school students taking the Scholastic Aptitude or the American College tests. The *bac* has been called "the national obsession of the middle class."

Among those who have earned the *bac*, some in the very top rank prepare for admission to the *grandes écoles* ("elite schools") rather than the universities. The *grandes écoles* train students for high-level careers in government, business, and industry. Admission is by an examination so rigorous that only one in ten passes. A few of the larger high schools offer a special postgraduate course of two or three years that prepares candidates for this exam. Those who fail are permitted to take it more than once.

A revealing anecdote is told about one female applicant who was taking the oral portion of the exam. She was so cool and self-assured that she had begun to annoy the jury of thirteen professors, business executives, and government officials.

Suddenly, to test her poise, a member of the jury asked: "Assume that you are a young diplomat; you are having dinner in the house of an African ruler; he tells the guests that various dishes containing human flesh will be served. What do you do?" Without batting an eye, the young woman replied: "I'd try it and then file a report." The jury burst out laughing—and approved her for admission.

The Universities

Until 1968, there were twenty-three universities. Many were over-crowded and understaffed. A major student revolt that year led to drastic reforms. The universities were reorganized into seventy-six smaller and more manageable units. Teaching methods, once highly formalized, with little contact between faculty and students, were re-shaped on a more flexible and democratic basis. New emphasis was placed on seminars and small classes.

Slightly fewer than a million students attend the universities. The Paris region alone has thirteen universities, accounting for one third of the total student body.

About 130,000 of the university students come from abroad, attesting to the worldwide reputation of French higher education. Roughly 60 percent of the foreign students are from Africa. Most come from France's former colonies, where they learned to speak French.

The universities automatically admit all applicants with a *bac.* The result of this open admissions policy is a high dropout rate—a shocking 40 percent in the first year. There are two main reasons. First, many students discover they cannot cope with the academic demands and personal freedom of university life. Second, many cannot afford to stay on long enough to earn the advanced degrees that have decent job prospects. Little financial aid is available.

To make the university system more realistic, two-year technical and business colleges were set up in 1966. These are specifically geared to employment possibilities, and *lycée* graduates are being directed toward them in increasing numbers.

The *Grandes Écoles*

The Ministry of National Education runs most of the 140 elite *grandes écoles*. Other ministries and some local chambers of commerce run the others. The oldest of the schools, the École Polytechnique (Polytechnical School), was established for military engineers during the Revolution. It is governed by the Ministry of Defense, though few of its graduates go into the armed forces.

Most of the *grandes écoles* are devoted to engineering, applied science, and management studies. The most prestigious include the École Nationale d'Administration (National School of Administration), the École des Hautes Études Commerciales (School of Advanced Business Studies), the École Nationale de la Magistrature (National School for Magistrates), the École des Mines (School of Mines), and the École des Ponts et Chaussées (School of Bridges and Roads).

Operating on a broader basis is a recently established *"super-grande école,"* the Institut Européen d'Administration des Affaires (European Institute of Business Administration), at Fontainebleau. Here a student body from France and some thirty countries spends ten to eighteen months studying international business problems and procedures. Instruction is given in three languages.

While admission to any of the *grandes écoles* is extremely difficult, the failure rate among their highly motivated and carefully selected students is almost zero. The curricula include individual research projects and practical experience in the field as well as formal lectures and theoretical study.

With employers eagerly seeking them out, the graduates are virtually guaranteed secure and lucrative careers at the topmost levels of French society. The 4,000 graduates of the École Nationale d'Administration since 1945 have included one president of the Republic, two prime ministers, dozens of cabinet ministers, hundreds of corporate executives and bank presidents. As an ENA official wrote in a recent magazine article, it is "a breeding ground for power."

A little more than a hundred years ago, *lycée* graduates were a rarity. Today 30 percent of the eighteen-year-olds attain the *bac*, and the number is rising. The amount of university students is five times greater than in the 1960s. The history of French education is a history of progress affecting ever-larger sections of the country's youth.

A Civilized Culture

French culture once dominated Western civilization. From about 1650 to about 1920, the upper classes in several countries preferred French to their own native languages. French was the official language for diplomatic negotiations and much government business. The achievements of French writers, artists, architects, and composers were widely admired and imitated. Since then, other cultures have moved to the forefront. English has overtaken French as the most widely spoken language.

Starting in the 1960s, the French became increasingly concerned about the invasion of their language by English words. *Le weekend*, *le snack*, *le fastfood*, *le drugstore*, even *le hamburger* are a few examples of this so-called *franglais* ("frenglish"). The new words first began to appear mostly in advertisements but soon spread into popular usage.

To counter this trend, a law was passed in 1977 outlawing foreign words—in all cases where perfectly usable French words existed—in all official documents, on radio and TV, and in ads.

Actually, the danger was probably exaggerated. Use of *franglais* has recently become much less chic than it used to be. Besides, the word borrowing works both ways. The English language has been importing French words and expressions for centuries.

Public concern about the purity of the language has not stopped the French from studying English as never before. Foreign-language study is compulsory in most schools and universities. Over 80 percent of French students have made English their first choice.

Despite such false alarms, French culture remains a vital and influential force in many parts of the world. Cultural creativity has never been livelier than it is in France today.

Until the late nineteenth century, the enjoyment and appreciation of literature and the arts were limited almost exclusively to aristocrats, the wealthy, and the educated middle classes living mostly in towns and cities. A relatively small percentage of the working class and the rural population could read or write. Few ever had the opportunity to visit a museum or art gallery or attend a concert. There was no radio or television to bring the fruits of human culture into the home.

Today, close to 100 percent of the people are literate. Free compulsory education was instituted in the 1880s, and every French child must now attend school until at least the age of sixteen. The percentage going on to universities and graduate schools keeps rising, partly because more scholarships are gradually becoming available. Newspaper and magazine circulation is way up. So are the number of permanent and mobile libraries and the number of books in circulation.

Music in all its forms draws large and enthusiastic audiences. There are more orchestras, more chamber groups, more opera performances, more singers, more players, more instruments owned and used by more individuals than ever before. Rock, jazz, disco, pop, all have their place, all have their stars and fans. Music schools have multiplied by 700 to 800 percent over the past quarter of a century.

Towns and cities in many parts of the country attract performers and audiences from all over the world to their annual festivals of theater, music, and dance.

Much of this cultural flowering has been a result of government support. In the 1970s about 0.5 percent of the national budget was allocated to the arts. That allotment doubled in 1987 and has since risen even further.

The Rise of French Culture

The achievements of French artists, writers, and composers are so numerous that descriptions of them have filled many books. Only a brief glance at some of the highlights can be attempted here.

In the Middle Ages, French artists produced mainly for the Church. They were best known for tapestries, illuminated manuscripts, stained glass, sculptures, and altarpieces in various forms. By the twelfth century the country's architects had invented the new Gothic style, soon to be imitated throughout the western world. Churches and cathedrals were designed with graceful pointed arches, slender spires pointing the way to heaven, and flying buttresses outside the walls to bear the weight of the roofs and allow for vast interior spaces. Outstanding among France's many magnificent Gothic cathedrals are Notre Dame de Paris, Chartres, and Rheims.

It was during the long reign of the *Roi-Soleil* ("Sun King"), Louis XIV (1643–1715), that French culture became preeminent in Europe. This period produced unique achievements in architecture, landscaping, design, literature, drama, painting, and music.

Many of the arts were brought together in Louis XIV's unrivaled palace of Versailles. With its stately and immense facade, its hundreds of magnificently decorated rooms, its great Hall of Mirrors, its spectacular gardens and fountains, it remains one of the world's most visited places.

Louis XIV also loved the theater, and in 1680 he established the Comédie Française for his favorite playwrights, Molière and Racine. This distinguished theatrical company has been the home of the French

IN THE PALACE OF VERSAILLES. *The Hall of Mirrors is one of the largest and most sumptuous rooms in the vast palace built by King Louis XIV. It was the scene of many extravagant banquets, balls, and other gala* fêtes.   Courtesy of French Embassy, Press and Information Division

classics ever since.

The eighteenth century is often described as the Age of Reason or the Enlightenment. The bold writings of the *philosophes* ("philosophers") have been discussed briefly in the section on the coming of the French Revolution (page 51). They challenged traditional beliefs about society and government. They asserted the rights of the individual against abuses of power by the king and the nobles. Life, liberty, and property, they contended, must no longer be subject to arbitrary seizures. Ancient superstitions and privileges must give way to science, the rule of reason, and the principle of human equality. The spread of such ideas paved the way for the French Revolution in 1789.

The *philosophes* also exercised a profound influence on America's Founding Fathers. Thomas Jefferson, for example, in drafting the Declaration of Independence, was aware of Jean-Jacques Rousseau's ideas about equality and the relations between the citizen and the state. The men who wrote the American Constitution incorporated Baron de Montesquieu's concept of the separation of governmental powers into three co-equal branches (executive, legislative, and judicial).

Toward the end of the eighteenth century, it was a French engineer-soldier who laid out the basic plan for the city of Washington, D.C. This was Major Pierre Charles L'Enfant of Paris, who fought alongside the American army during the Revolution. President George Washington invited him to design the nation's capital in 1791, and the magnificent result is universally admired to this day.

In the nineteenth century, writers and artists charted new directions. Romanticism was the dominant mode of thought in the early years. Romantic writers expressed deeply felt emotions and lofty idealism, extolled the beauties of nature, and reveled in the lure of faraway exotic places.

In the latter part of the century the Realists rebelled. These painters and authors insisted on depicting life honestly and without sentimental-

Four Philosophes

Charles de Montesquieu (1689–1755). *Persian Letters* (1721), *Causes of the Greatness of the Romans and Their Decline* (1734), *The Spirit of the Laws* (1748).

Voltaire (pen name of François Marie Arouet) (1694–1778). *English or Philosophical Letters* (1734), *The Century of Louis XIV* (1751), *Candide* (1759), *Philosophical Dictionary* (1764).

Jean-Jacques Rousseau (1712–1778). *The Social Contract* (1762), *Emile, or a Treatise on Education* (1762), *Confessions* (1781, 1782).

Denis Diderot (1713–1784). *Letter on the Blind* (1749), Editor of the *Encyclopedia* (1751–1772, 1776–1777, 1780).

Romantics and Realists

Stendhal (pen name of Marie Henri Beyle) (1783–1842). *The Red and the Black* (1831), *The Charterhouse of Parma* (1839).

Honoré de Balzac (1799–1850). *Eugénie Grandet* (1833), *Father Goriot* (1834), *The Human Comedy* (1842), *Cousin Bette* (1847), *Droll Stories* (1832–1837).

Victor Hugo (1802–1885). *Notre Dame de Paris* (1831), *Ruy Blas* (1838), *Les Misérables* (1862), *'Ninety-Three* (1874).

George Sand (pen name of Amandine Aurore Lucie Dupin, Baroness Dudevant) (1803–1876). *Lélia* (1839), *The Devil's Pool* (1846), *Jean de la Roche* (1859).

Gustave Flaubert (1821–1880). *Madame Bovary* (1857), *The Sentimental Education* (1874).

Emile Zola (1840–1902). *Thérèse Raquin* (1867), *Nana* (1880), *Germinal* (1885), *The Human Beast* (1890).

Six Impressionists

Camille Pissarro (1830–1903). *Markets in Rouen*, *Views of Paris*, *Quays of the Seine*, *Landscape Near Pontoise*.

Edouard Manet (1832–1883). *Race Course at Longchamps*, *Lunch on the Grass*, *Women on the Beach*, *The Bar at the Folies-Bergère*, *Olympia*, *In the Boat*.

Edgar Degas (1834–1917). *Ballet at the Opera*, *Blue Dancer*, *Dancers*, *Mlle. Fiocre in the Ballet* La Source, *Dance Rehearsal Hall*.

Claude Monet (1840–1926). *Impression: Sunrise*; *The Breakwater at Honfleur*; *A Lunch on the Grass*; *Camille, or the Lady in Green*; *Saint-Lazare Station*, *Terrace Near Le Havre*.

Pierre-Auguste Renoir (1841–1919). *Lise with a Sunshade*, *Woman with Fan*, *Madame Charpentier and Her Children*, *In the Loge*, *The Bathers*, *The Boat*.

Berthe Morisot (1841–1895). *Harbor of Lorient*, *Artist's Sister and Their Mother*, *Woman and Child in the Garden at Bougival*.

ity, often focusing on the lives of the common folk. They spurned the Romantics' mystical tendencies in favor of a naturalistic way of seeing life that was as scientific as they could make it. An earlier section in the historical chapters (page 71) includes analyses of works by two of the most important Realists, Honoré de Balzac and Émile Zola.

Starting in the 1870s, another upheaval in the arts resulted from the development of a new approach to painting called Impressionism. Young artists rejected the long-accepted, conventional ways of presenting reality. They too were fascinated by recent discoveries in science and experimented with new techniques for capturing the effects of light. Often they used tiny dabs of complementary colors, relying on the

DEAN OF THE PHILOSOPHES. *Voltaire fought tyranny and injustice with scathing wit and brilliant satires such as* Candide *(1759). Threatened with imprisonment, he lived much of his life in exile in Prussia and Switzerland.* By courtesy of the Board of Trustees of the Victoria and Albert Museum. Bust by Jean Antoine Houdon, 1781

viewer's eyes and mind to bring them together and form the desired effect.

The Postimpressionist painters of the late nineteenth and early twentieth centuries worked out new ways of seeing that were highly personal. They scorned the old emphasis on reproducing reality as accurately as possible. Instead, they sought to express their own innermost visions and emotions.

The public was first aroused to awareness of the new art by the Autumn Salon of 1905, an exhibition of works by young unknowns. Their slashing brushwork, raw colors, and daring rearrangements of space shocked one critic into calling them *Les Fauves* ("the wild beasts"). The name has been applied to them ever since. Henri Matisse

ONE DOT AT A TIME. *In this painting,* La Parade *("Invitation to the Sideshow") Georges Pierre Seurat (1859–1891) showed off the meticulous technique he had developed. It was called pointillism, because it used tiny points of color to create an overall effect.* The Metropolitan Museum of Art, Bequest of Stephen C. Clark, 1960. (61.101.17)

was their acknowledged leader. Others who subsequently attained enduring fame included André Derain and Georges Rouault.

Still another approach to painting was developed by the Cubists. They presented objects broken down into plane surfaces, viewed from several angles at once. This revolutionary new style was pioneered by Georges Braque and the Spanish-born Pablo Picasso, who came to Paris in 1904 and made France his home for many years thereafter.

Painters had no monopoly on the creative boldness that characterized Paris in the years around 1900. Writers and composers, too, were experimenting with new forms and visions.

A unique example was Guillaume Apollinaire, a poet and art critic who befriended the struggling modern artists and publicized and defended their work. In his own poetry he employed often playful new techniques to express the sensitivity of the artist in an unfeeling and materialistic world. One of his poems, which he called a "calligram," looked like this (in an English translation):

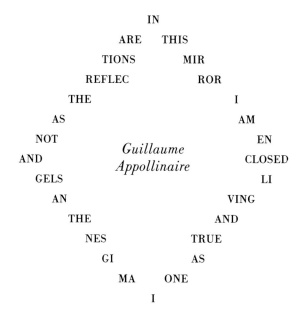

But creative artists needed patrons to provide both financial and emotional support. Unique among these was Gertrude Stein, an American writer who settled in Paris in 1903. She herself was only at the beginning of her eventual rise to fame as the author of works marked by experimental forms, most notably *The Autobiography of Alice B. Toklas* (1933) and the opera *Four Saints in Three Acts* (1934).

Stein was one of the first to purchase works by Matisse, Picasso, and many other artists of the time. Her apartment became a popular *salon*, where the most brilliant creators in every field gathered to gossip, exchange ideas, and benefit from her often insightful criticisms and advice. Several artists did portraits of her. The most famous was painted in 1905–1906 by Picasso, now in the collection of New York's Museum of Modern Art.

The horrors of World War I led to the development of an art movement called Dadaism, which emphasized the absurdities of life. Surrealism was another influential movement, reflecting psychoanalyst Sigmund Freud's discoveries of the roles of dreams and the unconscious mind in shaping behavior. Painters like Marcel Duchamp and André Derain and writers like Jean Cocteau, Louis-Ferdinand Céline, and André Breton exemplified these trends.

World War II produced a new generation of writers with its own distinctive point of view. Jean-Paul Sartre, probably the most influential thinker of the postwar years, expounded the philosophy of existentialism. Life was essentially absurd and pointless, Sartre said, yet human beings had free choice and were responsible for their actions. Nobel Prize winner Albert Camus expressed similar ideas in a series of brilliant, pessimistic novels.

Sartre's close companion for many years, Simone de Beauvoir, was a distinguished existentialist thinker in her own right. Her pioneering study *The Second Sex* (1949), which traces the history of women's oppression, has influenced feminist writers ever since.

The avant-garde among today's French novelists—Alain Robbe-Gril-let, Michel Butor, Nathalie Sarraute, for example—tend to reject the conventional elements of plot, storytelling, and character portrayal. Their works are difficult for the average reader and do not sell widely.

But there are others who write in the more traditional narrative vein: Henri Troyat, Jean Lartéguy, Gilbert Cesbron, and others. In 1980 historical novelist Marguerite Yourcenar became the first woman elevated to the Académie Française, the elite group responsible for preserving the purity of the French language.

Theater and Film

Paris has long been celebrated as one of the world's great centers of live theater. On almost any evening, its innumerable theaters and clubs present performances that range from bold avant-garde experimentation to risqué musical revues, from light comedies to eloquent renditions of French and world classics and to translations of modern foreign plays.

The provinces were regarded as a cultural desert for many decades. Live theatrical performances were almost impossible to find.

Today there are at least fifty theater groups functioning outside Paris. They provide some of the liveliest and most creative theatrical work done anywhere. Examples of their productions, along with others from around the world, can be seen at the annual summer festival of drama held in Avignon.

The French motion-picture industry too is flourishing. It produces about 150 full-length feature films a year, ranking it as the world's second filmmaker after the United States. The average investment in a French film is roughly one sixth the average investment in an American film.

French audiences generally enjoy American films. But in order to protect its own producers against the much larger and wealthier American industry, the French government limits showings of American imports to one third of those in the theaters. Half the films shown are French.

Though they are relatively little known to most of the American audience, French movies have included some of the world's most admired masterpieces. The first "golden age" of the French cinema occurred during the 1930s, in the memorable works of such directors as Marcel Carné, René Clair, and Jean Renoir.

A second period of rich creativity began in the late 1950s. It was called the *Nouvelle Vague* ("New Wave"). Its movies were often described as *films d'auteur* ("filmmaker's films") because they reflected their directors' personal styles instead of featuring big-name stars or lavish sets. François Truffaut, Claude Chabrol, Jean-Luc Godard, Eric Rohmer, and Alain Resnais were prominent among the New Wave directors.

Some of these men are still making movies. Other French directors who have created notable recent films include Louis Malle and Bernard Tavernier.

France's status in the world of film can be gauged from the fact that the most prestigious of the many film festivals held around the world every year is the one held at Cannes, on the French Riviera. Its awards are coveted by filmmakers of every nationality.

As in most developed countries, in France the spread of television has cut down on the size of the movie audience. Some 354 million tickets were sold by French movie theaters in 1960; only about half as many are sold today.

TV and Radio

France has six television channels. Three were owned and operated by the government until recently. These channels have been the prize in a tug-of-war between the Socialists and the conservatives in the government. The conservatives believe they should be privately owned and have already sold one of them. The Socialists favor government ownership.

Over 90 percent of French homes own TV sets, comprising about 10 million color TV sets and a roughly equal number of black-and-whites. The number of videocassette recorders and of stores offering videocassettes for sale or rental is multiplying fast. Viewers spend an average of thirty-two hours per week watching TV. The French also own home radios at a rate of one for every person—plus another 17 million in cars.

French TV and radio both have long-standing reputations for not being very exciting or innovative. The channels controlled by the government have little choice but to present the official point of view. News and public-affairs programs tend to avoid controversy or anything that might resemble criticism of the authorities. But the government channels do offer some excellent cultural programs.

The commercial channels emphasize light entertainment. About half the TV programs are imported, including several of the top-rated American shows.

The Heyday of French Music

French music first attained worldwide popularity in the nineteenth century. Composer Hector Berlioz (1803–1869), an ardent exponent of the Romantic spirit, pioneered the technique of telling dramatic stories and describing scenes from nature through orchestral music.

He won acclaim with his earliest major work, the *Symphonie Fantastique* (Fantastic Symphony) (1832). Berlioz was then passionately in love with an English actress, who spurned him. Berlioz poured his unhappiness into the symphony, portraying in musical terms the disturbing visions that he imagined would be experienced by a desperate young musician under the influence of opium. He embodied other romantic stories in subsequent works, such as *Harold in Italy* (1834), *Romeo and Juliet* (1839), and *The Damnation of Faust* (1846).

But for sheer long-lived popularity, no example of serious music has ever surpassed the masterwork of another nineteenth-century French composer. This is the colorful and richly melodic opera *Carmen* (1875), by Georges Bizet (1838–1875). Its melodramatic story of a gypsy girl, the toreador she loves, and the soldier who loves her in vain and ultimately kills her has enthralled audiences in every country where European operas are performed.

Where Berlioz and Bizet exemplify Romanticism in music, Claude Debussy (1862–1918) drew his inspiration from another nineteenth-century artistic movement, Impressionism. Like the painters of that school, he employed a delicate and inventive style to express the feelings and moods aroused in him by a given subject, rather than delineating the subject itself. His works include many brief pieces for piano such as *"Claire de Lune"* (Moonlight), *"La Cathédrale Engloutie"* (The Sunken Cathedral), and *"La Fille aux Cheveux de Lin"* (The Girl with Flaxen Hair), as well as symphonic works such as *L'Après-Midi d'un Faune* (*The Afternoon of a Faun*) and *La Mer* (*The Sea*).

The composer Erik Satie (1866–1925) adopted an even more eccentric approach. His works often contained elaborate jokes, as can be seen from some of their titles: *Three Flaccid Pieces (for a Dog)*, *Desiccated Embryos*, *Three Pieces in the Form of a Pear*, and *Five Grimaces*. Satie is probably best known as the composer of the score for one of the most innovative ballets of the period, *Parade*. With its startling scenery and costumes by Picasso, its scenario by the young poet Jean Cocteau, and its daring choreography by the celebrated star of the Russian ballet Léonide Massine, *Parade* was a sensational success.

In the field of dance, Romanticism had captured the imagination of French choreographers in the early nineteenth century. Of the many

GRAND OPERA. *(Above) At a nineteenth-century performance of Giacomo Meyerbeer's* Robert le Diable *("Robert the Devil"), an elegant audience throngs the magnificent auditorium of the Paris Opera.* The Dance Collection, New York Public Library at Lincoln Center

DANCERS IN ACTION. *(Right) In a painting of a dance sequence in the same opera, Impressionist Edgar Degas gave a close-up view of the audience and the dancers.* The Metropolitan Museum of Art, Bequest of Mrs. H.O. Havemeyer, 1929. The H.O. Havemeyer Collection, (29.100.552)

beautiful ballets conceived at this time, two are still among the most widely performed: *La Sylphide* (1832) and *Giselle* (1842). But this fruitful period was followed by nearly a century of decline in the creativity of French ballet. The best dancer-choreographers sought employment outside the country. Most notable of these was Marius Petipa, who became *premier danseur* ("principal male dancer") of the Imperial Russian Ballet in 1847 and first ballet master in 1869. Petipa's un-

matched career with the Russians lasted until 1903. He created a long list of ballets for them, several of which are still popular today (*Sleeping Beauty*, *La Bayadère*, and the perennial favorite *The Nutcracker*). Classical ballet since then has been based on the terminology and techniques invented by Petipa.

In France, it was not until 1929 that a dance company found a leader who inspired it to first-rank achievement. This dazzling performer and brilliant choreographer was Serge Lifar. In an outstanding career of nearly thirty years, he transformed the ballet company of the Paris Opera into one of the world's finest.

The Thriving World of French Music Today

France has never known such widespread musical activity. Sales of pianos, as one indicator, are six times greater than they were in the mid-1960s.

A new department of music was established in the Ministry of Culture in 1966. Within a dozen years the state budget for musical activities had multiplied six times. Government support made possible the creation of twelve new provincial orchestras, an equal number of provincial opera companies, the building of new conservatories, and the modernization of existing ones.

France's most distinguished composer-conductor, Pierre Boulez, had worked abroad for many years because conditions in his native country were unfavorable. In 1977 President Georges Pompidou set up a highly specialized new center, the Institut de Recherche et de Coordination Acoustique/Musique (Institute for Acoustical/Musical Research and Coordination), and brought Boulez to Paris to head it. The Institute now attracts students from around the world for research and experimenta-

OPERA GALA. *An opening night at the Paris Opera brings out the colorfully uniformed Garde Républicaine to do honor to the dignitaries descending the magnificent stairway.*
Courtesy of French Embassy, Press and Information Division

tion with electronic and other new forms of music.

Pompidou also appointed a dynamic new manager for the Paris Opera. It had been declining for years. Brilliant and daring new productions were mounted, and the world's top singers were brought in. Nowadays the Opera is 98 percent full at almost every performance, and it once again attracts a sophisticated and fashionable audience.

The leading opera houses in the provinces are those of Strasbourg, Lyons, and Toulouse. Several provincial cities host international music festivals during the summer. The biggest takes place at Aix, in Provence.

Musical life in France is by no means limited to highbrow programs. Jazz has long had a special appeal for the French. Many American jazz musicians have lived and worked in France for extended periods, basking in enthusiastic welcomes. Their way of life was movingly depicted in the 1987 film *'Round Midnight.*

According to the popular French magazine *Paris-Match*, there has been a "veritable explosion of rock among fourteen- to eighteen-year-olds." Rock concerts draw huge crowds, and records sell millions of copies. But the fans are not mere spectators; they are players too. There are over 25,000 rock groups.

After a long absence from the French schools, music was introduced as a regular part of the curriculum in the late 1970s. It has a long and difficult road ahead. Whereas 83 percent of American secondary schools have orchestras, only 8 percent of French schools do.

A Wave of Museum Building

By their number and variety, the museums of France rank among its chief cultural glories. About 15 million people visit them every year. Most famous of all is the vast Louvre, in the heart of Paris. Housed in a former royal palace, it displays artwork of all lands and many centuries. Leonardo da Vinci's painting *Mona Lisa*, the *Winged Victory of Samothrace*, and the *Venus of Milo* are only three of its world-renowned works.

More surprising is the glass pyramid designed by renowned architect I. M. Pei, which has towered over the main entrance to the museum since 1987. It produces a rather startling effect in the courtyard of the stately seventeenth-century palace.

Huge as it is, the Louvre is undergoing an expansion that will make it the world's largest museum by the end of the century. The plan is to move the Ministry of Finance out of the palace's immense north wing. Louvre collections that could not previously be shown will then be placed on exhibition.

More museums and cultural centers have been built since the 1960s, in more towns and cities throughout the country, than in any comparable period of French history. Two of the new structures, erected in Paris, have drawn strong reactions.

The Pompidou Cultural Center, popularly known as the "Beaubourg," opened in 1977. It has a unique architectural feature: the brightly colored pipes and ducts for its electrical, plumbing, and heating systems are in full view, on the outside of the cube-shaped building. The Beaubourg's startling look produced considerable shock and criticism at first, but it has become the most popular site in France. Seven million people visit it each year, while only 4 million visit the former number-one tourist attraction, the Eiffel Tower.

Inside, the Beaubourg's galleries display mostly contemporary art. Also contained within it are a library and concert halls. Street entertainers perform almost continuously on a broad plaza outside.

Another major museum opened in Paris in 1986. This was the Musée d'Orsay, set in a refurbished building that had once been the city's largest and most splendidly decorated railroad station and hotel. Its unmatched collection of nineteenth- and early twentieth-century French paintings features many world-famous Impressionist and Post impressionist masterpieces.

Quartered in a more traditional Paris mansion is the almost equally new Picasso Museum. It contains over 3,000 pieces from the artist's collection of his own work.

The Lively Press

Paris's eleven daily newspapers have traditionally been considered national, since they are distributed and read all over the country. But recently their readership has been declining. It dropped 3 percent in a single year, 1987. Today the French read half as many newspapers as the Americans, West Germans, Belgians, Austrians, Dutch, and Australians. Yet the French and Americans were the world's most avid newspaper readers before World War I.

In the mid-1970s the evening tabloid *France-Soir* was the best-seller, with over a million readers. Its circulation now hovers just above the 300,000 mark.

Le Monde (*The World*) too has been hard hit. Long regarded as the most liberal and distinguished of all the French papers, it had tripled its circulation from the late 1950s to about 1980, surpassing all the other Paris newspapers. Then it began to slide, dropping from a peak of over 500,000 readers to a low of about 350,000 today.

The conservative *Le Figaro* is the chief rival of *Le Monde. Le Figaro* had a much lower circulation around 1980 but now sells approximately 400,000 copies.

A notable recent trend has been the rise in popularity of the provincial newspapers. *France-Ouest* (*France West*), published in Rennes, the capital of Brittany, has attained the country's largest circulation by far.

Some of the former newspaper readership has gone over to the weekly newsmagazines. Most popular is *Paris-Match,* which features photojournalism and resembles the U.S. *Life* magazine.

The oldest and biggest of the traditional newsmagazines is *L'Express*, which is comparable in style and outlook to such U.S. newsweeklies as *Time* and *Newsweek.* Its leading left-wing competitor is *Le Nouvel Observateur* (*The New Observer*).

But of all the magazines published in France, none even comes close to the TV weeklies. The biggest is *Télé 7 Jours* (*TV 7 Days*), with over 3 million readers.

The Expanding World of Books

As the number of high school and university graduates rises, so does the number of books borrowed from libraries or purchased. The soaring demand has made publishing the largest cultural industry. Some 26,000 titles are published annually. Books on practical subjects and current affairs are the most popular, along with novels of romance and adventure.

Comic books outsell them all. A whopping 17 million copies are sold each year. There are about 1,000 different titles.

On the more serious side, literary competition is keen. Over 700 prizes are given each year. The most highly esteemed are the Goncourt, the Fémina, the Renaudot, the Interallié, and the Médicis.

Public libraries are not as common as in the United States or Britain. Only about 1,000 exist, though the number is rising. Most French books are purchased in bookstores or other retail outlets or by mail. A high percentage are quality paperbacks.

French Language and Culture Overseas

Though less widely spoken than in the eighteenth and nineteenth centuries, French remains one of the most important languages in the world. An estimated 120 million persons in forty-one nations and territories on almost every continent speak it as their first language. Over 200 million more use it regularly.

In Europe, French is the official language of all or part of Belgium, Luxembourg, Switzerland, and Monaco. It has official status in France's five overseas departments, as well as in twelve African nations that were once French colonies. Ten other African countries give French equal official status with another language. In the Americas, French is the official language of Canada's province of Quebec, of Haiti, and of French Guiana.

French is also a widely used language of instruction. This is only to be expected in former French colonies like Algeria, Vietnam, Laos, and Cambodia. But it is also true in countries where France once predominated and still wields considerable influence, such as Egypt, Lebanon, and Syria. A world wide "Association of Universities Partially or Entirely of French Language," has its headquarters at the University of Montreal.

In 1986 the governments of French-speaking countries formed an organization that they named *La Francophonie*. It meets annually to deal with world problems and to plan projects in agriculture, communications, cultural exchange, education, and scientific research. It hopes to achieve major international stature equal to that attained by the British-led Commonwealth of Nations.

Books in French are sold worldwide. In 1984 overseas sales earned over F 1 billion ($167 million), about one eighth of total book receipts. Textbooks were the biggest sellers, but every category of book found a market.

The French press, too, has an international readership. Four weekly newsmagazines (*Paris-Match*, *L'Express*, *Le Point*, and *Le Nouvel Observateur*) publish international editions. Some 2,300 other publications, including daily and weekly newspapers and periodicals, are sold in 110 countries. Over 2,000 publications in French are published outside France. L'Agence France Presse is the biggest French news service, but the demand for news in French is such that there are thirty-four lesser ones as well, serving the press all over the world.

Summing up, cultural activity in France today is lively and varied. Most critics agree that there has been somewhat less creativity in the visual arts than in earlier times. The level of originality and the depth of insight in literature and music may also have diminished. But France's cultural institutions have developed tremendously, bringing the finest fruits of the human mind and heart within easy reach.

There exists another revealing indication of the esteem in which the French hold their cultural heritage. No other country in the world has named so many streets, avenues, boulevards, and plazas after its artists, scientists, writers, and composers.

Advancing Science and Technology

The Great Tradition

From the physical sciences to medical research, from outer space to an undersea tunnel, French scientific and technical enterprises have ranged over the entire spectrum of human ingenuity. They have often produced advances that held major significance for the progress of humanity's knowledge and mastery of the world—and that have begun to reach out to worlds beyond. Every French government of the past 350 years has supported scientific and technical research. The first state-funded research establishment was the Jardin du Roi (Royal Garden), set up in 1635. It had hothouses, laboratories, and an amphitheater for lectures. It became a center for studies not only in botany, but in chemistry and astronomy as well.

In the 1660s, King Louis XIV organized the country's leading scientists into the Royal Academy of Science. In that age of geographical exploration, attention centered on problems of navigation. The king therefore assigned his new society a difficult task: measuring the precise length of a degree of longitude. The effort required far-flung expeditions and astronomical observations. The investigators scored the first triumph for organized French science by finding an accurate solution.

Count Georges de Buffon took office as superintendent of the Royal Garden in 1739. He set out the results of his vast researches in the thirty-six–volume *Natural History* (1744–1788). It shed light on the history of the earth and presented a mass of evidence for the evolution of species.

The eighteenth century also witnessed the publication of two great multivolume works that summed up all existing knowledge in science and technology. One was the *Description and Perfection of the Arts and Vocations*, edited by the naturalist and physicist René Réaumur. Its 121 parts began to appear in 1761. The other was the thirty-six–volume *Encyclopedia*, edited by Denis Diderot and published over the period stretching from 1751 to 1780.

ENLIGHTENMENT SCIENCE. *This engraving from the Encyclopedia shows experimenters at work in a well-equipped eighteenth-century chemical laboratory.* From Denis Diderot and Jean d'Alembert, eds., *Encyclopedia (Recueil des Planches),* (Paris, 1762–1772)

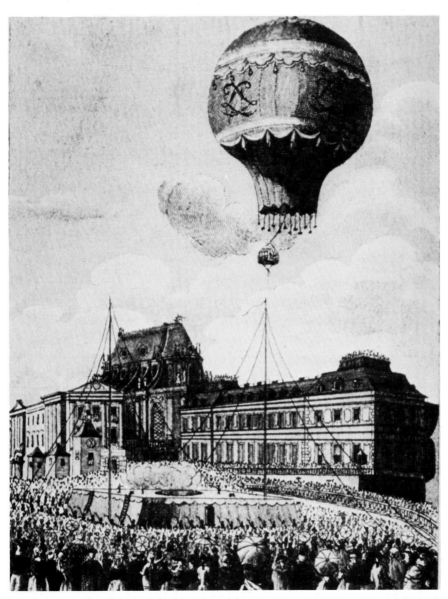

AVIATION PIONEERS. *The Montgolfier brothers achieved the world's first manned balloon flight in June 1783. As seen here three months later they were invited to demonstrate their "Aerostatic Machine" to King Louis XVI and the royal court at Versailles.* Courtesy of French Embassy, Press and Information Division

For one of the most brilliant scientists of that era, there was tragedy. Antoine Lavoisier is revered today as the founder of modern chemistry. His most significant achievement was the discovery of a new element, which he named "oxygen." Lavoisier proved that oxygen was the key to the process of combustion.

But Lavoisier accepted appointment as a tax collector for the king. During the Revolution, such former royal officials were regarded as enemies of the people. Lavoisier was guillotined in 1794.

The First Medical Breakthroughs

All through human history, efforts to heal the sick and treat the injured were hampered by unproved theories and faulty techniques. Around 1800 a new spirit arose among physicians and medical researchers. They began to emphasize clinical observation, laboratory experiments, and the collecting of facts instead of empty theorizing.

French medical men were among the leaders of the new movement. Marie François Bichat (1771–1802), for example, was the first to carry out detailed anatomical studies of the tissues that form the organs of the human body. Claude Bernard (1813–1878) conducted physiological experiments that revealed the functions of the pancreas and the liver.

The greatest of all nineteenth-century French medical researchers was Louis Pasteur (1822–1895). He was actually a chemist rather than a doctor. Investigating several plant and animal diseases that were threatening agriculture, he showed that they were caused by microorganisms, or germs. Pasteur's findings laid the foundation for the germ theory of disease, opening the way for modern medicine.

One of the most seriously affected branches of agriculture was wine making. Germs were souring many types of wine. Pasteur discovered that the simple process of heating the wines to a temperature of

FATHER OF MODERN MEDICINE. *Louis Pasteur (1822–1895) revolutionized medical science by proving that microorganisms, or germs, cause many diseases. He developed vaccines for anthrax in sheep and rabies in dogs and humans.* From René Dubos, *Louis Pasteur, Free Lance of Science* (New York: Charles Scribner's Sons, 1976)

131° F (55° C) killed the germs without affecting the taste or aroma of the wines. The process was named after him: pasteurization. It has been routinely applied to many products since then, especially milk and dairy products.

Pasteur was then drawn into the study of a disease that affected both animals and humans: hydrophobia, or rabies. He had developed a cure for it in animals when a young boy who had been bitten fourteen times by a rabid dog was brought to him. The lad's mother begged Pasteur to administer the new drug, for death was certain otherwise.

But the drug had never been tested on humans. Pasteur went through an anguished crisis of conscience. Finally, moved by the boy's terrible suffering, the scientist reluctantly consented. Over a period of fourteen days he injected vaccine containing the rabies virus. He started with weak doses and built up to dangerously powerful ones.

Blessedly, Pasteur's vaccine worked. Within the next two years, 1,250 children were treated successfully at his laboratory.

The painstaking methods worked out by Pasteur for the study of disease and the development of treatments became models for generations of researchers.

Recent Medical Progress

One of the world's foremost research centers, the Pasteur Institute in Paris, now carries on the courageous chemist's work. Its leading research team recently shared a historic breakthrough with a team of American specialists that was working on the same problem at the same time. Both teams independently isolated the AIDS virus and developed a blood test for it.

In 1987 an immunologist at the Pierre and Marie Curie University in Paris developed a possible vaccine for AIDS. He took the bold step of injecting himself and several volunteers with it. Tests showed that their bodies raised immune defenses against two strains of the AIDS virus. Years of clinical verification would be necessary before these promising results could be confirmed.

A team at the Tours medical school scored a major achievement when it developed a vaccine against hepatitis B, a widespread form of liver infection. Other Tours scientists have demonstrated the use of ultrasound techniques to measure the flow of blood in the arteries and organs—even in fetuses—as a way of fighting thromboses (blood clots).

In Paris, medical-school researchers have discovered the cause of hypertension (high blood pressure). Their findings allow precise diagnosis and early detection of this common and often deadly illness.

Ominous Discovery: Radioactivity

In 1891 a young student of physics and chemistry came to Paris from Poland. Her name was Maria Sklodowska, but she was to become world-famous under her married name as Marie Curie.

Working with her husband, the French chemist Pierre Curie, she investigated the mysterious process of radioactivity. The young couple's pathbreaking studies resulted in the discovery of two radioactive elements, polonium and radium. They won the most coveted award in all of science, the Nobel Prize, in 1903. Their work opened the new fields of nuclear physics and chemistry.

Pierre Curie died in 1906, but Marie carried on alone. Her research on radium and its compounds won her a second Nobel Prize in 1911.

The Curies' daughter Irène, too, was an outstanding physicist. Like her mother, she married and worked closely with a French scientist, Frédéric Joliot. And again like her mother, in 1935 she shared the Nobel Prize with her husband. The Joliot-Curies had synthesized new

Some Notable
Recent French Achievements

MEDICINE

Vaccines against influenza and hepatitis B

Isolation of AIDS virus and perfection of test for detecting it

New chemical synthesis of Vitamin A

ENERGY

First nuclear-waste-treatment plant

Super Phenix, world's most powerful nuclear-energy generator

TRANSPORTATION

World speed record for railroad trains: 238 mph (380 kph)

Driverless, computer-controlled urban train

OCEANOGRAPHY

Nautilus and Jean Charcot, world's most fully perfected undersea research vessels

TELECOMMUNICATIONS

Second place in world market (after U.S.) for space satellites

MILITARY TECHNOLOGY

RITA "super-field-telephone" system, purchased by U.S. Army

Mirage, Jaguar, and Super Étendard jet fighter planes

Crotal and Exocet, world's most widely marketed missiles

Rubis, world's smallest nuclear submarine

radioactive elements. Though they may not have foreseen it at the time, their work was one of the major steps that led within a few years to the discovery of nuclear fission and the development of nuclear weapons.

France in Space

The French space program dates from 1961. That was when the government set up the Centre National d'Études Spatiales (National Center for Space Research). Its headquarters were located in Toulouse, the long-established hub of French aviation.

The new center's scientists and engineers first developed a series of satellites for use in telecommunications and meteorology. These had to be carried into space by American rockets. The French experts then began working out designs for their own rocket.

The fruit of their efforts was Ariane. Its first successful launching took place in 1979. By 1983 Ariane was placing telecommunications and meteorological satellites into orbit. These included U.S.-made Intelsat 5 satellites.

Some of the French satellites have demonstrated unexpected military uses. Spot, a civilian satellite, made headlines in July 1987 when it discovered and photographed a secret Soviet nuclear-submarine base above the Arctic Circle.

The year 1980 saw the establishment of Arianespace, the world's first commercial company for space transportation. The French provided 60 percent of the funding, with thirty-six European companies and thirteen banks sharing the rest.

Successful launchings continued in the mid-1980s. Soon Arianespace was exulting in a backlog of orders for forty-six satellite launchings from fifteen clients, with fees totaling about F 15 billion ($2.5 billion). Then came the disaster of May 1986, when an Ariane went out of control and had to be destroyed.

The accident occurred just five months after the explosion of America's Challenger shuttle, with its seven astronauts all killed. Both countries had to suspend launchings for many months while every detail of their space-vehicle designs and equipment was checked and reworked.

Ariane was first to get off the ground again. The redesigned rocket, 160 feet (47.4 meters) tall and weighing 240 tons, carried two satellites into orbit in September 1987. By that time it had cornered one half the world market for commercial launchings. French astronauts have ridden with Soviet cosmonauts on two space missions. The most recent lasted thirty-eight days. By special request, the astronauts' food was prepared by French chefs.

Meanwhile, plans were already under way for construction of the first European space shuttle, Hermes. Sponsored by the fourteen-nation European Space Agency, it was to be almost entirely French designed and French built. The 20-ton Hermes was to carry four to six astronauts and a 4.5-ton payload. Its first flight was scheduled for the mid-1990s.

Columbus, a French-built European space station, was expected to follow Hermes into orbit before the turn of the century. By the time it is completed, France will have spent an estimated F 100 billion ($16.7 billion) on its total space effort.

The Channel Tunnel

The prime ministers of France and Britain concluded a historic agreement early in 1986. They agreed to build a tunnel beneath the English Channel, forming the first physical link between their two countries.

SPACE SHUTTLE. *The first flight of Hermes, the French-built, European-sponsored shuttle, is planned for the mid-1990s. The sketch shows how it will place satellites into orbit.* Courtesy of French Government Tourist Office

Called Eurotunnel by its sponsors, it has been nicknamed the "Chunnel" by American journalists. Such a tunnel has been dreamed of since at least the time of Napoleon.

Several designs had been submitted. The ultimate choice was a railway tunnel, with twin tubes for shuttle trains carrying cars, trucks, and passengers. A third tunnel between them will permit service and maintenance. Electricity has been chosen as the trains' power source, easing the difficult problem of ventilation in such a long tunnel.

The tunnel will connect the two countries at the narrowest point of the Channel. It is to extend for 31 miles (50 kilometers), from a point just south of Calais, on the French coast, to Cheriton, south of Dover in England. Nearly four fifths of its length will lie 132 feet (40 meters) below the sea bottom. Each of its two railway tubes will have a diameter of 24 feet (7.3 meters).

The trains will each carry 200 cars or 35 trucks at a top speed of 100 miles (160 kilometers) per hour. The trip will take 30 minutes. France's 170-miles-per-hour (270-kilometer-per-hour) high-speed train system will eventually be extended to and through the tunnel—and even into England as far as London.

Work on a tunnel project had actually begun back in 1975, but the British changed their minds and withdrew. The idea of ending their island's separation from the European continent was hard for them to accept. Digging had already progressed several hundred meters on each side when it was halted.

But the new agreement, signed in 1986, was ratified by the two parliaments the following year. Work resumed at once, employing about 20,000 people. They excavated from both ends. Eleven giant boring machines, each weighing nearly 1,000 tons, each more than 100 meters long, and each worth $10 million, ground their way forward at the rate of eighteen feet a day. The two teams were expected to break through in 1991, with the tunnel opened to the public two years after that.

Though supported and strictly supervised by both governments, the tunnel's $7.4 billion financing was raised entirely from private sources.

France's "Science City"

The French are keenly aware that their country's future depends on accelerating progress in science and technology. They are turning that conviction into a unique reality.

The reality takes the form of a scientific-technical town called Sophia Antipolis. Founded in 1971, the complex covers a previously untouched area one fourth the size of Paris, between Nice and Cannes on the Riviera. It comprises three settlements of 500 buildings each. Its diverse facilities already employ several thousand people and are creating an average of 700 new jobs each year.

Sophia Antipolis brings together an awesome concentration of over 110 government and private research centers and future-oriented industries. Among them is Europe's largest center for solid-state technology and another for solar-energy studies. Notable among the internationally known American companies represented are Digital Computers and Dow-Corning. Air France has a facility, in a fortresslike bunker, capable of handling worldwide reservations.

The French Commitment to Science

Government funds support the National Center for Scientific Research, in Paris. With a broad variety of programs in many branches of science, history, and the social sciences, it is France's largest such institution. Its annual budget has risen in recent years to about F 7.5 billion ($1.25 billion).

A National Research Institute on Computer Science and Control was recently set up in a Paris suburb. Its staff of 800 ranks among the world's leaders in the highly sophisticated fields of artificial intelligence and robotics.

French scientists also participate in the investigations of subatomic particles conducted at the European Center for Nuclear Research, in Geneva. They are building a huge particle accelerator at Caen, in Normandy, that will enable the international scientific community to pursue these studies with deeper insight than has previously been possible.

In 1980 the national budget for basic scientific research totaled F 14.5 billion ($2.4 billion). Today it exceeds F 40 billion ($6.7 billion), nearly 2.5 percent of the gross national product. France's investment of so large a share of its GNP in science places it fifth among the world powers, after the United States, the U.S.S.R., West Germany, and Japan. The nation is determined to enter the twenty-first century in the front rank.

The New Life-Styles

Into the Cities— And Out of Them

Not so long ago, France was a nation of rural peasants and small-town dwellers. But people started moving out of the countryside in ever-mounting numbers in the 1950s. Since then the nation has transformed itself into a highly urbanized society. Seven out of ten now live in towns, cities, and suburbs. Nearly 12 million live in the Paris region alone.

Since 1975, however, there has been movement in the opposite direction as well. The 1982 census showed that the big towns were no longer attracting new inhabitants and were even losing some. Towns of less than 20,000 people, including many suburbs, had the biggest growth rates.

Over half the urban population now lives in new suburban houses or housing developments. As happened in the United States and other countries, many of the new developments built until about 1972 were mistakenly planned as huge high-rise complexes. These crowded facilities often tended to deteriorate into slums fairly quickly.

Since 1972 new planning and design systems have created *villes nouvelles* ("new towns") in and around the older centers. These developments are smaller, as are the buildings that form them. They are also more carefully integrated into the existing communities.

An interesting change is the smaller number of cafés in the new towns. This is doubtless due at least partly to new antialcohol laws limiting the number of cafés to one per 3,000 inhabitants.

Up to the late 1950s and early 1960s, cafés and bistros remained the main centers of social life—mostly for men, less so for women. Here the men of the villages and *quartiers* ("neighborhoods") would gather for coffee, drinks, light snacks, and lively, endless talk. The custom has certainly not disappeared altogether; it has simply lost some of its former popularity.

In the cities, certain cafés still specialize in specific types of clientele. There are literary cafés, artists' cafés, musicians' cafés, students' cafés, and many others. In Paris, for example, the Café des Deux Magots and the Café Flore, in the St.-Germain-des-Prés *quartier*, have long been famous as gathering places for the city's intellectuals.

But the French seem to feel less need for cafés today than they once did. Their newer, larger, more comfortable apartments, their TV sets and other amenities have lowered the drive to go out. Nowadays they tend to visit each other at home much more than in the past. Young people in particular have abandoned their fathers' old café habits for other preferred hangouts, such as clubs, discothèques, even the new shopping malls.

A recent poll showed the extent of the change. Only 15 percent of

PHILOSOPHER AT WORK. *Jean-Paul Sartre, Existentialist thinker and playwright, sets down his ideas at a table in his favorite café on the Left Bank in Paris.* The Springer/Bettmann Film Archive

the population now go to restaurants once a week, but 83 percent prefer to invite their friends over for dinner at home.

Over half of all French families own their own homes or apartments. Large numbers have been buying up old farmhouses or building villas in the country as second homes. These serve for weekends, summer vacations, or retirement. The French hold the world's record for ownership of second homes: one family in nine owns one. The comparable figure in the United States is 1 in 15, in Germany 1 in 140, in Britain 1 in 200.

The 1982 census also revealed a trend that Americans can appreciate. French families were deserting the northern and eastern regions for the milder climates of the south and the shore.

Family Life

As long as France was predominantly a rural country, most people lived in extended families. Three or even four generations would live together in big country houses.

Over the past half century the extended family has been disappearing as the French—especially the younger generation—have moved to the towns and cities. The nuclear family, comprising only parents and children, is now the norm. Urban living, with most families in apartments, provides little space for the old-fashioned way of extended family togetherness.

This change was not accomplished without considerable strain. In the first years after World War II, the country faced a severe shortage of housing. Large families had to stay together, often in crowded conditions. The shortage has now been resolved. Thousands of housing units have been designed and built to accommodate nuclear families, with separate housing developments for the elderly.

Fathers and grandfathers had ruled French families for centuries.

Their authority was accepted without question. Under the Napoleonic Code, the legal system established in the early 1800s, women were totally subject first to their fathers and then to their husbands.

Upper-class women were expected to serve as adornments in the home. At most they might participate in cultural life by maintaining a *salon*, converting the home into a meeting place for the intellectual elite.

These traditions are changing. Families are becoming more democratic. Recent legislation has considerably broadened the rights of women and children.

The trend has affected public life as well. The French tend to be far less formal than they once were. There are fewer ceremonial banquets, with old-style formal speeches. Informal entertaining in the home has become the favored way. People use first names more freely—though perhaps not quite as freely as Americans do.

A major factor promoting change was the Matrimonial Act of 1964. Before that, a wife had to get her husband's permission if she wished to open her own bank account, own and manage a shop, or get her own passport. The law freed married women to perform these and many other activities as the equals of men.

Other changes in the status of women have further loosened family ties. More women are working than ever before. Many have built major professional or business careers. Some 15,000 women started their own businesses in a single recent year.

Further evidence of women's changing attitudes was contained in a 1987 poll that showed that 85 percent of French women (as opposed to 76 percent in 1981) feel that politics can no longer be left to men exclusively. Only 13 percent stated that they automatically vote as their husbands do.

As would be expected in a Catholic country, divorce was traditionally difficult and expensive to obtain. But the moral authority of the Church has weakened in recent years. A law passed in 1975 made it possible to arrange a divorce by mutual consent. About one marriage in five now ends in divorce, and the number is rising. The wife is almost invariably granted custody of the children.

Like most advanced Western countries, France has experienced a sexual revolution since the 1960s. Respectable unmarried couples seldom lived together before that time. Such behavior was regarded as scandalous. Today, four out of ten couples live together before marrying. On the average they stay together two years. This has taken the place of the old-style formal engagement.

Laws against birth control were repealed in 1967. Abortion was legalized in 1974. The number of abortions has been high.

Nouvelle Cuisine

French cooking has been celebrated as the Western world's finest since the sixteenth century. Recipes prepared in the traditional style of *haute cuisine* ("high-style cooking"), as developed by such renowned chefs as Jean-Anthelme Brillat-Savarin (1755–1826) or Georges Auguste Escoffier (1847?–1935), are still featured in distinguished restaurants. This style features meats and fish prepared with thick sauces containing high-calorie ingredients, such as cream, egg yolks, sugar, brandy, flour, and other starches.

Today's concern with dieting and health has produced a new style of cooking. *Nouvelle cuisine* ("new cooking") has gradually been winning public favor. It emphasizes lighter, subtler tastes, requiring the best and the freshest raw materials. In cooking meats, for example, its chefs use only the natural juices, without added sauces.

The methods and techniques of *nouvelle cuisine* are said to have been invented by a chef named Paul Bocuse, who runs a famous restaurant in Lyons. The term itself was created by two well-known food critics,

Henri Gault and Christian Millau. They publish a widely used guide to the restaurants of France.

At the end of World War II, a badly battered France had more urgent concerns than catching up with the lifestyles of less damaged, more affluent societies. Now it has just about done it, slowly and painfully at first, but finally with impressive speed and its own unique brand of *joie-de-vivre* ("joy of living").

The Consumer Boom

The average French home has been filling up with consumer goods. The following table shows the percentage of families that owned various types of durable goods at various times since the 1950s. It illustrates France's sharply rising standard of living.

Percentage of French Families Owning Durable Goods

	1954	1970	1984
AUTOMOBILE	21.0%	56.0%	72.0%
REFRIGERATOR	7.0%	79.0%	96.4%
FREEZER	0.0%	0.0%	32.8%
DISHWASHER	0.0%	2.0%	20.6%
WASHING MACHINE	8.0%	55.0%	82.7%
TV *(any type)*	1.0%	69.0%	91.2%
TV *(color)*	0.0%	0.0%	61.4%
TELEPHONE	37.8%	51.1%	80.0%

A steady rise in purchasing power since about 1960 made it all possible, raising the country to twelfth position in worldwide standard of living. France stands above the average in western Europe.

Frenchwomen have always been admired for their seemingly instinctive sense of style in clothing. The growing affluence of middle-class and working-class women has enabled them to indulge in ever more refined tastes. Fashion magazines such as *Elle* and *Marie-Claire* have never been more popular than now. They have further heightened women's sense of elegance.

Haute couture ("high fashion") clothes, because of their astronomical prices, have always been restricted to a few thousand rich society women. Well-designed, well-made, ready-to-wear clothes were uncommon until recently. Nowadays the latest fashions are copied and mass-produced at reasonable prices almost as soon as they appear. It is often hard to tell a woman's socioeconomic status by her clothes.

The Retail Revolution

Until the 1950s, French consumers had to do most of their shopping in the small stores that still dominated the retail trade. And yet it was a French retailer who had already invented the department store way back in 1852. The first, called Bon Marché (Good Value), opened in Paris in 1852. It still exists, as do those that soon followed: Au Printemps (Springtime), Galeries Lafayette (Lafayette Galleries), and many others. Later, chains of stores selling cheaper goods spread through the country: Monoprix and Prisunic are the best known.

The first supermarket, an idea probably picked up from the Americans, was established in 1957. Today, nearly 5,000 of them sell over 60 percent of the packaged foods.

Recent years have seen the birth of a new concept, the "hypermarket." With a huge selling space, it combines the department store and the supermarket. Some of the newest ones, such as the Carrefour company's new hypermarkets outside Marseilles and Fontainebleau, are bigger than any American stores.

Carrefour plans to build two hypermarkets in the United States. Au Printemps too is joining the trend. It opened a branch in Denver in 1987 as a first test of the U.S. market.

ULTRA-SHOPPING MALL. *The gleaming glass-and-steel forum of Les Halles tops the triple-level underground mall and recreation center recently built on the site of an old-time marketplace in central Paris.* B. Annebicque/Sygma Photo News

The Leisure Boom

As late as 1966, most offices and factories worked a five-and-a-half-day week, including Saturday morning. Public schools held classes all day Saturday, though they usually closed on Wednesday or Thursday. It was only when Saturday became a day off in many enterprises and schools that the French began to discover the joys of weekends. The leisure boom was born.

The gradual stretching of annual vacations has given the boom an added lift. Vacations averaged two weeks in 1936, three weeks in 1956, four in 1965, and five since 1981.

Over half of all families now vacation away from home. One out of four vacationers goes abroad. Spain is the most popular destination. Some 350,000 French tourists visited the United States in a recent year.

Personal spending on leisure activities has more than quadrupled since 1950. *Le camping* is very popular, with an estimated 7 million families taking to the countryside. They can choose among a half dozen recently established national parks and twenty-two regional ones. France's many excellent beaches draw an estimated 46 percent of all vacationers. Topless sunning and swimming are almost universally accepted.

A long-standing, stubborn problem has made for crowded resorts and a virtual economic standstill at vacation time. Four out of five French vacations are scheduled between mid-July and the end of August. As any summertime visitor to Paris can confirm, it is hard to find any French people there, other than those who serve tourists, or to get much normal business done during those weeks.

The government has campaigned for staggered vacation periods, but it has had little success so far. Attempts are under way to make a start on uprooting this deeply ingrained pattern by rearranging the school holidays. Adult vacations could then be planned accordingly.

Disneyland Comes to France

EuroDisneyland is coming! Construction began in 1988 on a
5,000-acre development in Marne-la-Vallée, twenty miles (thirty-two
kilometers) east of Paris. The new amusement center will feature
not only the Magic Kingdom, Westernland, Adventureland,
Fantasyland, and other attractions familiar to Americans, but new
ones specifically geared to catch the imaginations of Europeans of
all ages. Charles Perrault's *Mother Goose Stories* may be dramatized,
for example. The life of Napoleon is another possibility.

The complex is due to open in 1991. It will include hotels,
campgrounds, shopping, dining, and entertainment areas, as well as
outdoor recreation facilities. Over 10 million visitors are expected
each year. Disney movies have always been popular throughout
Europe.

Six villages in the area, with 4,500 inhabitants, will be affected.
But the French and American planners intend to leave the quaint
old buildings, village squares, and cafés intact.

Investors in France, Europe, and around the world are joining
the Disney Company in financing EuroDisneyland. Ownership and
management are French.

Euro Disneyland

© 1987 Disney

The Sports Boom

As their leisure time has expanded, the French people have gone sports happy. In 1975 an estimated 11 million persons were registered in all forms of organized sports. The number has now zoomed to 17 million, or nearly one third of the population. There are about 130,000 sports clubs and associations.

Individual sports draw the biggest numbers. About a third of all sports participants swim, ride horseback, play tennis, ski, climb mountains, or sail. One in six favors team sports, such as *le football* ("soccer"), basketball, and volleyball. Soccer is the most popular, with nearly 2 million amateur players.

Interestingly, though French soccer fans do support their teams enthusiastically, they tend to be less passionately partisan that those of other countries. Even at hard-fought international championship games, there have been none of the riots, the drunken rowdiness, or the fighting that have marred games elsewhere.

Tennis ranks second. About 1.3 million men and women play, and 160,000 of these have earned rankings from the French Tennis Federation. France is the only country in the world to hold more than 3,000 tennis tournaments each year.

Skiing stands third in popularity, with over 800,000 registered enthusiasts. They do not have to travel very far, for France boasts the world's largest total area of "skiable" surfaces. More than 500 ski centers are located in the Alps, the Pyrenees, the Jura, the Vosges, and the Massif Central. The excellence of these facilities won France the privilege of hosting the Winter Olympics of 1924 at Chamonix, those of 1968 at Grenoble, and those of 1992 at Albertville, all in the Alps region.

A less conventional French specialty is flying. The country boasts

DOWNHILL DAZZLE. *A skier hits the slope at Flaine, one of the many recently developed Alpine resorts in France.* Courtesy of French Embassy, Press and Information Division

35,000 licensed pilots and 12,000 trainees—a high figure for a population the size of France's. They log about a million hours of flight per year. A quarter of their flying is done in gliders. Ultralight planes are the newest rage. France already has 3,000 of them.

The sports fad has captured people of every age. Streets and roadways have blossomed with thousands of joggers and walkers from tiny tykes to valiant oldsters.

Along the *autoroutes* ("superhighways"), many of the rest areas have been expanded into *étapes sportives* ("sports stops"). They feature tracks for running, obstacle courses, and all sorts of exercise equipment. Motorists can now relieve the boredom of long trips with enjoyable, healthful body-building breaks.

Women, too, are playing and exercising as never before, though their numbers still lag behind those of men. The women are getting into sports previously regarded as exclusively masculine: basketball, judo and karate, soccer, skydiving, motorcycling, even boxing. French-women have won championships in auto racing, judo, wrestling, soccer, and bicycle racing.

Their skill and stamina on bicycles have improved so impressively

The Tour de France: An International Craze

Imagine the Super Bowl and World Series combined. The result would create about as much excitement as the Tour de France does throughout western Europe.

Created in 1903, this annual bicycle race carries a vast stock of legends, spectacular achievements, and immortal names. French riders have won in most years, but foreigners have occasionally earned the right to wear the coveted *maillot jaune* (''yellow jersey'') that honors the victor. An American, Greg LeMond, triumphed in 1986.

The Tour is run during the first three weeks of July. The course extends over 2,400 grueling miles (4,000 kilometers). It roughly follows the country's borders, forcing the cyclists onto some of the world's steepest, most muscle-wearying mountain roads.

About twenty teams participate each year, making up a total of 180 to 200 riders. The winner is the rider who finishes the course with the lowest total time. About 40 percent drop out along the way.

Some 20 million cheering fans line the route. The TV audience for the finish, on the Champs-Élysées in Paris, has been estimated at a stupendous 800 million people.

that an annual 595-mile (991-kilometer) Tour de France race has been set up for women. It provides a female alternative to the long-established Tour de France for men.

The sports boom is all the more remarkable considering that French schools have only recently begun to include physical training and sports in the curriculum. Part of the reason was that education authorities traditionally believed that the schools should focus solely on academic

TOUR DE FRANCE. *The grueling annual bike race, with teams from many countries, mesmerizes millions of European fans. Its 2,400-mi (4,000-km) course takes 23 days to complete.* Copyright Disney

training. But it was also true that many schools lacked facilities such as gymnasiums, stadia, tennis courts, playing fields, or swimming pools.

Since the 1960s, there has been an almost explosive sports building boom. Municipalities all over the country have built sports venues. Public swimming pools were a rarity until the 1960s. Today every town has at least one. All the new facilities are made available to the schools as well as the general public.

Professional sports have benefited too. Seven major soccer stadia have been constructed in as many major cities. Each of the new stadia accommodates about 50,000 fans.

Paris has received its own sparkling new indoor sports arena, the Bercy Omnisports Palace. This ultramodern structure adapts with ease to sports ranging from boxing to tennis, from horse shows to hockey games, from bike races to basketball. It seats 11,000 to 14,000 spectators.

The French are determined to improve their standing in international competitions, especially the Olympics. Their concern is evidenced by the recent establishment of the National Institute for Sports and Physical Education, just outside of Paris.

Here the various sports federations send their top athletes. Six hundred of them, from fourteen to twenty-five years old, receive skilled and rigorous training geared to world-class competition. The National Institute is backed up by regional centers and national schools that specialize in specific sports.

It was not until the mid-1980s that France had built up the infrastructure required for successful competition in every field against the world sports powers. Now it is ready. It will be heard from.

Eternal France, Ever-Changing France

Suppose that a Frenchman of 100 years ago has been transported into the France of today. He finds much to amaze him—but also much to reassure him.

Above all, he finds his people pretty much as he left them. He recognizes their qualities: highly individualistic, skeptical, logical yet profoundly emotional, not very respectful of government or authority in any form, yet still capable of passionate involvement in politics. He is pleased to find that they love their country as fiercely as ever.

More surprising to him is the new mix of racial and ethnic elements. The resulting tensions disturb him. But he is encouraged by the efforts under way, by government and by private groups, to promote harmonious intergroup relations.

Looking around for familiar buildings, the visitor from the past finds the best of them carefully preserved. Parts of many towns and cities, mostly the central areas, hardly seem changed at all.

He need not look far, however, before being awed by the sheer volume of new construction. Looming up all around him are the new residential developments called *villes nouvelles* ("new towns"), the vast industrial complexes, the gleaming high-rise office buildings. He marvels at the superhighways and high-speed rail lines, but these he can understand. They are just modernized and expanded versions of the roads and railways he remembers from his own time.

But when he is shown the airports around the urban centers and when he sees and hears the jets thundering through the skies, these alarming novelties have to be explained to him. A visit to the great aerospace center at Toulouse enlightens him, though it leaves him dazed at first.

Soon he is reminiscing about the science-fiction classics of one of his favorite French authors, Jules Verne. A hundred years ago, Verne predicted many of the wonders our visitor is encountering.

Taken on a tour of France's many nuclear-power plants, he probably thinks of them as belonging to the same science-fiction category.

Our visitor asks what products all those factories are producing. Is France still world renowned for its incomparable wines, its delectable cheeses, its exquisite perfumes, its superb high-fashion clothes?

"Mais oui!" his well-informed guide reassures him. All these are still in demand on the world market. But France has developed way beyond them. It is now competing successfully against the best that other nations can offer in high technology.

Roaming through the countryside, the visitor falls in love all over again with the timeless beauty, the endless variety of the French landscape. He soon notes that the lush farmlands are even more productive than he remembers them. He wonders at first why there seem to be fewer peasants at work. The answer quickly becomes plain: Their places have been taken by powerful machines. The consolidated farms on which the machines operate are much bigger than the small holdings that were common in the old days.

While traveling through the provinces, the visitor asks about cultural life outside Paris: Is it still as barren as in his own day? He is dazzled as he is shown the many new provincial museums, the Maisons de la Culture, the theaters and opera houses and concert halls—all bustling with activity and patronized by increasingly knowledgeable and enthusiastic local audiences.

Inevitably, the old-timer wants to visit the schools he had attended. Remembering the strict formality and sometimes harsh discipline of his time, he is fascinated by the new classroom democracy. Instead of the old passive ways of learning, the old emphasis on memorizing long lists of facts, students are participating actively in the education process. They are interacting with computers, carrying out scientific experiments, doing field studies.

Work in all subjects is conducted at new high levels, but science and technology are drawing infinitely more attention than in the past. France is determined that its young people shall be fully prepared for the twenty-first-century world they will live in.

Very different changes impress him when he pays some family calls. He remembers growing up secure in the bosom of a large, extended family in a spacious country house. There were grandparents to dote on him and cousins to play with. Now most families comprise only parents and children, living in city apartments or smaller houses.

But the families seem happy in new ways. Father or grandfather are no longer the absolute rulers. Women have come a long way toward equality. Even the children share in family decisions.

And those new homes! The visitor gapes in wonder at the technical marvels that fill not only millionaires' homes but those of workers too. Doesn't anyone do anything by hand anymore?

And what do the family members do with all the spare time gained for them by the wonderful new appliances? Back in our visitor's youth, work filled the waking hours. Leisure was for rich people.

He learns that today's families have time to enjoy life in ways undreamed of not so long ago. They have their choice of forms of entertainment in the home. They take advantage of their recently freed weekends and newly prolonged vacations to travel, to share in the nation's rich cultural life, to practice sports in greater numbers than ever.

The visitor is surprised by the high proportion of elderly men and women among the general population. He recalls how things were back in the late nineteenth century. The number of Frenchmen and -women who lived past forty in those days was much lower than it is now.

It is welcome news to him that the people's health is greatly improved, that first-class medical care is available to all, and that these factors have helped lengthen people's lives.

Finally, and eagerly, the visitor turns toward Paris. Is it still the City of Light, the magical, magnetic city that the whole world loves to call its second home?

He first seeks out the Place de L'Étoile (Plaza of the Star), the great circular plaza topped by Napoleon's mighty Arc de Triomphe (Arch of Triumph). He ticks off the names of the twelve stately avenues that radiate from the Étoile. They remain unchanged.

He turns his gaze down the broad avenue leading eastward from the Arch, the Champs-Élysées. He is relieved to find that its splendid vista still leads through the Place de la Concorde to the Tuileries gardens and the Arch of the Carousel.

But he is perplexed to discover that the Étoile has been renamed Place Charles de Gaulle. A quick lesson in twentieth-century history is

PARIS BY NIGHT. *A one-quarter-size model of the Statue of Liberty (the full-size Statue was a gift of France to the U.S.) stands on an island in the Seine. The Eiffel Tower looms behind it.* Courtesy of French Embassy, Press and Information Division

called for, explaining to this nineteenth-century man who de Gaulle was.

When he turns to face westward from the Arch, the time traveler is astounded by what he sees. There, off in the distance, rearing up over what had been flat and tranquil Neuilly, stands a gigantic assemblage of steel-and-glass towers.

The agitated visitor is informed that this is the new La Défense complex. It is a carefully planned mix of office towers and residential buildings. Badly overcrowded Paris has long needed such a development. Better to erect it on the outskirts of the capital rather than somewhere in its heart. Well, *peut-être* ("perhaps"), he grudgingly allows. It is certainly impressive.

The visitor glances over toward Montparnasse on the Left Bank. He asks irritably why an office tower over seventy stories high had been permitted there, well within the city? A mistake, he is told. Since it was built, no more skyscrapers have been permitted inside the city proper.

Strolling through Paris, our visitor expresses his gratification: the city is as hauntingly beautiful as ever. Only its pace is much more hurried than he remembers.

Yet there are more changes to get used to.

He can hardly help a gasp of amazement when he comes to Les Halles. Until recently Paris's huge main food market had occupied this site in the very center of the city. For decades it had been the cause of monumental traffic jams, as hundreds of trucks converged on the area.

The old market has disappeared. Les Halles is now an ultramodern, triple-level, underground shopping and recreation center. It even contains an Olympic-size indoor swimming pool. At street level it is crowned by a lovely park surrounded by graceful glass-and-steel archways and arcades.

At the Place de la Bastille, where the French Revolution began in 1789, he inquires about the spectacular modern structure that now dominates one side of the big plaza. He is told that this is Paris's newest opera house, the Opéra de la Bastille. Audiences have grown so large that the city's two world-famous opera houses no longer suffice. This new people's theater presents opera at popular prices. *"Quelle idée magnifique!"* ("What a magnificent idea!") the visitor exclaims.

Next, the time traveler is conducted into the Métro (subway). He recalls that such a system had been discussed in his day but never built. Its quiet running is explained, its rubber-tired wheels pointed out. He

TRADITION. *In this timeless photograph taken on a road in Provence, in southern France, a father and son bring home the* baguettes *(crispy loaves of French bread).* Courtesy of French Government Tourist Office

admires the beautifully redecorated stations that reflect their locations. The one below the Louvre Museum, for example, displays works of art.

At last, the visitor is granted a moment's respite. He relaxes at a sidewalk café, munches some delicious *canapés* of *pâté de foie gras* ("goose-liver sandwiches"), sips a refreshing Pernod, observes the colorful scene.

"*Eh bien,*" he declares with a contented sigh, "much has changed in France. And, *grâce à Dieu* ("thank God"), much remains the same. When I was young, we thought we had reached the pinnacle of progress. Now I realize how far the world still had to go. People living today are lucky.

"And yet, we too were lucky. Our joys were perhaps simpler than yours, yet we treasured them. We had not seen the terrible wars and disasters of your time.

"Would I prefer to go back to my world, or stay here?" He has to reflect a while on that one.

"But you see, *mon ami* ('my friend'), it wouldn't make that much difference. I believe I could find happiness in any era. I propose only one condition: Whether I return to my past or stay in your present, I am ready to live anywhere—so long as it is in France!"

Suggestions for
Further Study

Books

If you wish to consult another general survey of France, Time-Life's *France* (1984) is vividly written and abundantly illustrated. Younger readers can enjoy either Dominique Norbrook's colorfully illustrated *Passport to France* (New York: Franklin Watts, 1986), or the charming *France*, by Peter Moss and Thelma Parker (Chicago: Children's Press, 1986). Able readers will find a rich fund of information in Irish scholar John Ardagh's *France in the 1980s* (Harmondsworth, England: Penguin, 1983). Ardagh has also produced a well-illustrated region-by-region survey, *Rural France: The People, Places, and Character of the Frenchman's France* (Salem, Mass.: Salem House, 1983).

Russell Miller's exciting *The Resistance* (New York: Time-Life, 1979) was written specifically for teen-agers. Preteens may prefer Don Lawson's *The French Resistance* (New York: Messner, 1984). A fuller account is *Resistance: France, 1940–1945*, by Blake Edwards (Boston: Little, Brown, 1965). The story of the 1944 battle for Paris is dramatically recounted in *Liberation*, by Martin Blumenson (New York: Time-Life, 1978).

The man who led the Resistance, General Charles de Gaulle, has been the subject of numerous studies. Susan Banfield's *De Gaulle* (Edgemont, Pa.: Chelsea House, 1985) will satisfy most teen-age readers. For a more detailed and scholarly analysis, you might try Jean LaCouture, *Charles de Gaulle* (New York: Holmes & Meier, 1987).

Histories of France are so numerous that only a few specialized works can be listed here. A readable survey, with well-chosen illustrations, is *The French Kings*, by Frederick C. Grunfeld (Amsterdam: Time-Life, 1983). Helpful for understanding the mighty Charlemagne in the context of his time, though written for adults, is Donald Bullough's *The Age of Charlemagne* (Bridgeport, Conn.: Merrimack, 1973). Susan Banfield's sensitive *Joan of Arc* (Edgemont, Pa.: Chelsea House, 1985) is another of her books for teen-age readers. *Saint Joan of Arc*, by Victoria Sackville-West (Boston: G. K. Hall, 1984), is a beautifully written full-length biography. Of the many studies of Louis XIV, one of the richest and most enjoyable is Nancy Mitford's *The Sun King* (New York: Harper & Row, 1966).

Few subjects have been more written about than the French Revolution. Susan Banfield's *The Rights of Man, the Reign of Terror: The Story of the French Revolution* (New York: Harper & Row, 1989) tells the story from the ground up, including changes in fashions, festivals, and food. Robert and Elizabeth Campling have prepared a brief account for secondary school students, *The French Revolution* (North Pomfret, Vt.: David & Charles, 1984). Christopher Hibbert's adult *Days of the French Revolution* (New York: Morrow, 1981) sympathizes with the radicals.

Two of the many biographies of France's first emperor can be recommended for young adults: Manfred Weidhorn's *Napoleon* (New York: Macmillan, 1986) and Donnali Shor's *Napoleon Bonaparte* (Morristown, N.J.: Silver Burdett, 1986).

Equally readable is Alistair Horne's copiously illustrated *The Terrible Year: The Paris Commune, 1871* (New York: Macmillan, 1971). Gifted students interested in another watershed event of the nineteenth century cannot do better than Jean-Denis Bredin's massive and masterly *The Affair: The Case of Alfred Dreyfus* (New York: George Braziller, 1986).

Studies of French culture explicitly designed for young readers are hard to find. One of the most fascinating of the adult works is *Bohemian Paris: Culture, Politics, and the Boundaries of Bourgeois Life*, by Jerrold Seigel (New York: Viking, 1986). The role of an eccentric but influential American writer in the evolution of modern French culture is interestingly told in *Charmed Circle: Gertrude Stein and Company*, by James R. Mellow (New York: Praeger, 1974).

If you are intrigued by the French way of life, two highly readable sources will enlighten you: *Growing Up in France*, by Sabra Holbrook (New York: Atheneum, 1980), and *We Live in France*, by James Tomlinson (New York: Bookwright Press, 1983).

Serious students of present-day France will find stimulating and candid opinions by a distinguished French politician in *The Trouble with France,* by Alain Peyrefitte (New York: Knopf, 1981).

Cookbooks

Enlightening on many subjects, as the subtitle indicates, is *Classics from a French Kitchen: Delicious, Simple Recipes, Both Ancient and Modern, Together with Savory History and Gastronomic Lore in the Grand Tradition of the Cuisine of France,* by Eliane Ame-Leroy Carley (New York: Crown, 1983).

"Good cooking doesn't mean complicated recipes or expensive ingredients. The simpler the food, the better, in my opinion." So says Paul Bocuse, the chef usually credited with inventing *nouvelle cuisine,* in the introduction to his *Paul Bocuse in Your Kitchen: An Introduction to Classic French Cooking,* translated and adapted by Philip and Mary Hyman (New York: Pantheon, 1982).

Films

Feature Films

Even a brief selection of film classics—including silent movies of the 1920s—can provide incomparable insights into the French people and their history. One of the most remarkable is *Bonaparte and the Revolution*, Abel Gance's lengthy romanticized epic (235 min., b/w, silent; Images Film). Students curious about surrealism will be enriched by experiencing Jean Cocteau's allegory *The Blood of a Poet* (63 min., b/w, silent; Texture Films).

Of the many fine films created by the great director Jean Renoir, two stand as imperishable achievements. *The Grand Illusion* (111 min., b/w; Kit Parker Films) is a moving testament to the human spirit in wartime. *The Rules of the Game* (110 min., b/w; Budget, Corinth, Films Inc., Janus) is a brilliant study of upper-class decadence.

The film trilogy *Fanny*, *Marius*, and *César* (120 min. each, b/w; Budget, Corinth, Kit Parker), based on the novels of Marcel Pagnol, portrays life in Provence in warm and humorous fashion. New Wave director François Truffaut's first film, *The Four Hundred Blows* (98 min., b/w; Janus), tells the poignant story of a youngster driven into delinquency by parental neglect. The aristocracy of the Revolutionary era is sharply depicted in *La Nuit de Varennes* (150 min., color; Swank).

An American film that depicts in gripping fashion a shocking true incident affecting the French army in World War I is *Paths of Glory* (87 min., b/w; MGM United). Collaboration and resistance during the German occupation of France in World War II are the subjects of a unique documentary, *The Sorrow and the Pity* (260 min., b/w; Cinema 5).

Educational Films

The titles of the following films are self-explanatory. They represent only a small sampling of the vast selection that is available.

France—Yesterday and Today (20 min., color; Associated Instructional Materials)
Joan of Arc: A Profile in Power (25 min., color: Learning Corp. of America)
A Portrait of Molière (62 min., color; French-American Cultural Films)
French Revolution: Death of the Old Regime (17 min., color; Britannica)
French Revolution: Birth of a New France (21 min., color; Britannica)
Napoleon: The Making of a Dictator (27 min., color; Learning Corp. of America)
Napoleon: The End of a Dictator (26 min., color; Learning Corp. of America)
The Origins of Art in France (40 min., b/w; Roland)
Impressionism and Neo-Impressionism (22 min., color; International Film Bureau)
Fauvism (17 min., color; International Film Bureau)
Paris: La Belle Epoque (24 min., color; Media Guild)

Videocassettes

The Middle Ages (31 min., color; International Film Bureau)
The Crowning of Charlemagne (19 min., b/w; Univ. of Toronto)
The Sun King (30 min., b/w; Indiana Univ.)
Versailles (55 min., color; Media Guild)
Voltaire Presents Candide: An Introduction to the Age of Enlightenment (34 min., color; Britannica)
The Guns of August (110 min., b/w; International Historic Films)
Open Air: Monet and the Impressionists (28 min., color; Univ. of Toronto)
Claude Debussy (28 min., color; International Film Bureau)
Dada (31 min., b/w; International Film Bureau)
Marc Chagall: The Colors of Passion (24 min., color; International Film Bureau)
France: The Socialist Experiment (25 min., color; Journal Video)

Records

The following are all 33⅓ rpm long-playing records.

Distinguished contemporary figures in the arts and sciences discuss their lives and careers, in a series called *Français de Notre Temps.* Two sides are devoted to each individual.

Medieval music comes alive as H. Cuenod sings *French Troubadour Songs* (2 sides,

Chesterfield). Cesare Valletti sings songs by Fauré, Debussy, and others in *French Art Songs* (2 sides, RCA). *French Folk Songs* (2 sides), *French Folk Songs for Children* (2 sides), and *Songs of the Auvergne* are excellent collections by Folkways.

Eighty songs demonstrate the love of the French for their capital city in *Paris Je T'Aime* (2 sides, French-American Cultural Service). *Parisian Swing* features classic French jazz artists Django Reinhardt, Stephane Grappelly, and the Quintet of the Hot Club of France (2 sides, GNP Crescendo).

Two interesting sets of readings are presented in *French Poetry* and *French Prose*, both read by Prof. J. V. Pleasants (2 sides each, Goldsmith). Folkways has put together stories by Voltaire, Maupassant, Mérimée, and others in *French Short Stories, Vols. I and II* (2 sides each).

Audiocassettes

A varied collection grouped under the overall title *French Songs* includes *The Charles Aznavour Story* (30 min.), *Folk Music of France* (30 min.), *France's Folk Songs* (30 min.), *French Patriotic Songs* (15 min.), *Let's Sing Songs in French* (30 min.), and *Patachou at Carnegie Hall* (30 min.) (Univ. of Colorado).

Similarly, readings collectively titled *French Language and Literature* present actors and native speakers performing excerpts from Balzac, Baudelaire, Racine, Molière, Verlaine, and others (60 min. each, BFA Educational Media).

The most popular of all French operas, Bizet's *Carmen*, is available in many recordings.

French men and women from various walks of life tell their stories in the *How They Live* series (15 min. each, Univ. of Colorado).

Index

Numbers in *italics* refer to illustrations.

St. Malo, 98
St.-Michel, Mont, *96*
St.-Michel-d'Aiguihle, *94*
St. Nazaire, 98
St. Paul, 101
St. Tropez, 99
St.-Victoire, Mont, *102*
Sand, George, 172
Saône River, 112
Saracens, 32, 101
Sarraute, Nathalie, 178
Sartre, Jean-Paul, 177, *207*
Satie, Erik, 181
Scholastics, 37
schools, 223
    nursery and primary, 160–61
    secondary, 161–64, *162*
"Science City," 203
Seine River, 87, 95, 112
Senate, 152–153
Seurat, Georges Pierre, *175*
Seven Years' War, 50
sexual revolution, 210
skiing, *217*
social security system, 157
Socialists, 82, 148
solar energy, 130, *130*
Sophia Antipolis, 203
SOS Racism, 21–23, *22*
space program, 199–200
sports, 216–20, *217*, *219*
Statue of Liberty, *225*
Stein, Gertrude, 177
Stendhal (Marie Henri Beyle), 172
Strasbourg, 90, 108
student uprisings (1968), 79–80, *81*
subway, 143, 226
Super Phenix, *129*
Surrealism, 177

Tavernier, Bernard, 179
tax evasion, 117
telecommunications, 145
Télé 7 Jours, 188
television, 179–80
Tennis Court Oath, 53, *54*
theater, *29*, 170, 178
Thiers, Adolphe, 69
Three Musketeers, The, 45
tidal energy, 130
Toulon, 100
Toulouse, 105, 136, 200, 222
Tour de France, 218–19, *219*
tourism, 92, 144
trade unions, 138
train, high-speed, 143–44, *143*, 202, 222
transportation, 142–44
Troyat, Henri, 178
Truffaut, François, 179
truffles, 104

unemployment, 16, 80, 95, 121, 140
United Nations, 75
United States, 74, 117, 136, 141, 150, 178, 213
    Constitution, 157, 171
universities, 164–65
uranium, 127–28

Valmy, Battle of, 56
Vandals, 30
Van Gogh, Vincent, 102
Vercingetorix, 28
Verne, Jules, 222
Versailles, palace of, 46, *170*
Vichy, 75, 94

Vietnam, 13, 78
villes nouvelles, 206, 222
Voltaire (François Marie Arouet), 172, *174*
Vosges Mountains, 89, *90*

Washington, George, 171
Watteau, Jean, 51
Weil, Simone, 79
Westphalia, Treaty of, 46
William the Conqueror, 35–36, *36*

wines, *104*, 134–35
women, *115*, 209, 212, 218–19
workers, *115*, 116–17, 138–40
    immigrant, *6*
World War I, 73–74, *74*
World War II, 1–10, 20, 75, 121

Yourcenar, Marguerite, 178

Zola, Émile, 71, 172